THE
PERFORMANCE ALPHABET

78 Quick Wins for Maximum Performance

Harmen Stevens

Recommendations for Harmen Stevens

"If you have ever worked with someone and wondered how they do it all so effectively, than you have probably worked with Harmen. He is a Leadership expert, a coach, an educator, a husband and father.

Harmen has the ability to make you feel like you are the only person present when he is speaking. He teaches you without feeling as you have been having nothing more than a conversation.

Being across the Atlantic from each other doesn't ever come into play because Harmen makes himself available and shows up.

Any individual or company that has the ability to work with Harmen should. The results are amazing and having him in your corner even more so."
September 29, 2011

Judy Hoberman
Consultant / Coach / Speaker / Trainer / Author,
JH Endeavor / Selling In A Skirt

"Harmen has that special capabilty of making you feel like you can do anything. He is a true expert in the leadership and coaching field.If your lucky enough to work with Harmen you will come out ahead because he makes it his mission to help you be successful."

Mary Francis
Author and Public Speaker, The Sisterhood of Widows

"Harmen has a natural gift to communicate in a crisp clear & yet buzz-free way, though he can do that as well. When I attended one of his presentations […] he managed to shorten the distance to finding data I did not know yet.[…]"

Paul Van den Brande
Associated Partner, Just in Time Management Group

"I have just worked with Harmen as I was blocked at some point in my business.
I have been coached before though I noticed I didn't really act upon it afterwards. Harmen coached me yesterday morning and I have already taken action with great result!
He managed to guide me exactly to these action points I needed to continue.
Top and highly recommended!"

Sylvie Verleye
Owner at Presentation Academy Simply Talking

"I had to pleasure of working with Harmen, when he joined our team for the pre-launch of our Generous Networkers program.

He is one of those rare people, who are totally focused on helping others! A true giver! He goes way beyond the actual tasks at hand and shows outstanding responsibility. On top of that, Harmen provides fresh ideas and thinks in solutions.

He is definitely a great asset to any team!"

Bert Verdonck
LinkedIn Expert | Lifehacker | Networking Speaker | FREE Bestseller www.how-to-really-use-linkedin. com | Happy Chocoholic

"I have met Harmen during my work at Salaw Group. Harmen is a passionate coach and teacher. He is a natural. His coaching skills allow him to easely work with people, reach and energyze them.

I strongly recomend Harmen if world class coaching is what you need."

Horacio Jäkel
Partner at ABC Latinoamérica

"Harmen not only performed as a business developer (short AND long term succesfull projects in the pipeline), but on top of that he executed some projects whereby the clients expectations were far exceeded!

So I'm always happy and proud, and at ease, to propose Harmen to a client, knowing his expertise and professional state of mind always culminate in a major succes story!

Thanks Harmen!"

Michel Cuypers
Owner, Beconsult

"Harmen Stevens has an eye for achieving goals! Working with Harmen has been a fruitful enterprise, where excellent ideas emerge naturally!

His extensive experience in sales & leadership coaching and training make happy clients!"
May 20, 2010

Stephan Vanhaverbeke
Managing Partner, ubeon | business experts

"Harmen is a no nonsens guy, straight to the point , eager to learn. He knows what he wants and executes his projects efficient and fast."
June 16, 2010

Ides De Vos

"Harmen is a liable, dedicated, ambitious and positive person, which shows in a very good quality of his service.

It is a great pleasure working with him!"
March 25, 2011

Jeroen van Rooij
Health & Vitality management expert

"Harmen, is detail oriented and an asset to anyone's team. Working with Harmen you quickly find out he committed 100%.

Once the goal is accomplished he is ready for the next challenge!"

Jacob Roig
Master Business Success Coach, Loral Langemeiers Live Out Loud

edicated to

My wife and trusted partner, An,

Loral and Carl, for their unconditional support,

Ward, for his introduction to a new world,

Byron, for seeing things I didn't see in myself,

Clifford and Claire, for putting up with my British English,

My beautiful baby girls, Gwen and Maya, for just being there

And:

My team and my staff, I'd be lost without you,

All the experts I've had the pleasure of learning from,

I love you all

THE PERFORMANCE ALPHABET

78 Quick Wins for Maximum Performance

Harmen Stevens

Introduction

Socrates wrote: "All I know is that I know nothing."

Wise words, indeed. Continuous study of books on subjects like philosophy, history, current affairs, future possibilities, personal development, communication, success, sales, and leadership, has brought me to the same conclusion: the more I learn, the more I realize I still have much to learn.

Over many years, this realization has allowed me to reach a higher level of consciousness: recognizing patterns of human behavior, sequences of decisions that help or hurt businesses large and small, and seeing social trends that are currently transforming our society in ways that may or may not prove to be beneficial for future generations.

With regard to human behavior, the resilience of the human species gets tested daily. In just the last ten years we have had two major tsunamis causing hundreds of thousands of casualties, earthquakes almost beyond our scale of measurement, and major oil disasters. We have had economic downturns for which economists don't even dare predict when the recovery will actually start, as well as a continuing disintegration of the industrial society.

Encircling all these events, there is the Internet as a virtually unlimited source of quality information (along with a lot of misinformation).

Men and women in power are finding it harder and harder to explain to their constituents why government is moving so slowly while the world in general seems to be gaining speed. Humans behave differently nowadays than in the 20th century. They are more giving toward those they like, more critical about the people they associate with, more open to new opportunities, and more entrepreneurial than ever. This has absolutely nothing to do with what country they live in (with the exception of a few dictatorships, perhaps) or their culture.

Francis Fukuyama wondered in his masterful book, *The End of History and the Last Man*, whether there would ever be a concept that would surpass democracy (in the purest of its forms and far from the political use or abuse of the term in the last few decades) as a better solution for the continuing growth of the human species. Flying back from Berlin after a three-day conference in 2011, I had the good fortune to spend some time with a man who was active in an international think tank. I asked him how he saw it. He said there wasn't even a future political model better than democracy at the moment. What an eye-opener! People know more now than ever before, and yet the number of unknowns keeps growing. One can only wonder how this will change human behavior in the coming years.

As for decisions and sequencing, scores of books have beenwrittenonthesetopics.Ifinditextremelyfascinating to see how the management gurus of our time still use so many of the industrial-era types of decision-making models that were effective for the past two centuries. However, the biggest flaw in those models, as many of them secretly admit, is that they are based on the premise that human beings are a liability and intellectual capital cannot be valued in monetary terms on the asset side of a balance sheet. Meaning well, they say that society is not ready for that specific paradigm shift yet and tell their public to use the old way of thinking.

Poppycock.

Businesses have always been able to circumvent these paradigms, the best examples being the gurus themselves. Their business models are based primarily on applied knowledge and much less so on machinery or buildings. Well, ladies and gentlemen, your secret is out.

One of my mentors, Loral Langemeier, realized early on that her business is driven by sequencing her company in such a way that her clients bring their knowledge to the (Big) table and so everybody wins. For her it is about community, and she's making money on that value, whereas many of my friends in banking would think it a huge risk to invest money in her company BECAUSE of the fact that she has hardly any tangible assets compared to her industrial friends.

She sequences her values before her bottom line, her conversation before her conversion, and regards her team as her ultimate asset: as her family, rather than a liability. We should all learn from that.

In my view, the business decisions of the 21st century will, as my friends David Covey and Stephan Mardyks say, be value-driven. We are developing from a knowledge-based society to a value-based society. Business decisions will have less to do with the bottom line and more with "if" and "how" a decision is in line with the values that your business reflects.

Turning to the story I am about to share with you, Mr. Jones himself regards his team and staff as part of his family but also has a group of friends OUTSIDE his business environment that is able to help him out. His decision to have such a group is based first on his personal values, much less on the values in his business. You need both to succeed as a business person in this century.

Social movements have always had their place in history; every turnaround in society has had its movement. Lately, however, movements have taken their place in the realm of the virtual world. Elections are now won through a professionally run election campaign with both online and offline elements. I remember comments during the 2008 presidential election in the United States, when Barack Obama swept the floor with John McCain, a war hero who had proven himself many times over in the political arena called Washington, about the difference in strategy. It was said that John McCain's constituency clearly wasn't ready for the digital age yet and that the Obama campaign collected massive donations through the Internet.

Whether that's true or false is not for me to say. The fact remains that the conversation became real and present. Social movements are now as strong in the virtual world as they are in the actual world.

Social media platforms and the people who actively participate in them are doing business, supporting each other, becoming actual friends, and synergizing, from Brisbane to Brussels to Bakersfield, California.

I consciously do not touch on the subject of the virtual world in this book yet, as it would bring up some aspects of leadership and management that Mr. Jones would likely not be able to answer. His mental flexibility would probably allow him to lead his team, actual or virtual. Nevertheless I have consciously chosen NOT to combine the concept of Leadership with the complex matter that is the Internet, as my current knowledge on the subject has not yet reached a level where I feel comfortable having that conversation. Having said that, I realize that many of my online followers would likely disagree. For them I have the following words:

As I encourage you daily to take action and follow your values, so I expect my followers to encourage me to bring my virtual leadership to light.

When I feel that my leadership online has come to virtual adulthood, it will be the result of the great synergy I enjoy with all of you and especially with Gary Loper, my virtual go-to-guy whom I have never met in person. (Although I have a feeling we have worked together numerous times in another life. . .)

About the concept of this book: modeling has always been a large part of my success in business. My ability to adopt and adapt has brought me from rags to something beyond rags—I refuse to call it riches, as it is not at all in my style to brag about such things. What I can say is that by modeling alone, I have been able to achieve goals beyond my imagination, going from driving through Napa Valley in a Mustang Convertible (as a Belgian, California is a somewhat exotic place, trust me) to becoming a father of two beautiful baby girls to becoming an entrepreneur (not necessarily one of my first dreams—those were about flying without wings—but definitely the most fun dream) to becoming a coach to overcoming that constant pain in my lower back.

I have modeled successful people and businesses, allowing me to expand my network exponentially (yes, also in the actual world), learning from and working with the best. My strong point has always been my ability to DO something with what I've learned, so I would like to invite you to do the same.

Hence the idea of modeling businesses and people based on 26 conversations with an imaginary Mr. Jones instead of just one or two long interviews. As any manager knows, you can always find ten minutes in a day, no matter how busy you are.

Mr. Jones is loosely based on the different types of managers I have met and worked with over the years—including some portion of myself, although I have to admit Mr. Jones has a better sense of humor and likes to play mind games a little bit more.

The ABC-coach is based on the many strong women I have met in the last few years, including my mentor Loral Langemeier (also known as the Millionaire Maker). Her relentless energy and focus on results and teamwork has more than once saved my behind. I sort of imagine my fictional character as being at the beginning of her career and trying to find her own way into the business of doing business.

The conversations of my characters have a strong evidence-based tone, so I have also opted to leave out a lot of descriptive narrative where possible to guarantee the quickest possible intake of information for you, the reader. For it is you who is important, not Mr. Jones, nor the ABC-coach.

Some final points to bear in mind as you read:

Mr. Jones received a questionnaire from the ABC-coach immediately after the call in chapter 1 so he could prepare the different letters of the alphabet for their interviews.

Yes, both characters are modeled after numerous people I have actually met—so sorry, it's not coincidental.

Yes, some of the stories are based on my own experience.

No, I don't use spiral notebooks – I use mindmapping on my tablet.

Yes, we are preparing more books on the subject of ABC-modeling.

And yes, we are still looking for models (always wanted to say that).

Hopefully you will have as much fun reading as I had writing. And, as Loral would say:

GO, GO, GO. . .

Harmen Stevens
Beerse, Belgium, July, 2012

BC

Success is that old ABC—ability, breaks, and courage.

~ Charles Luckman

"Hello, am I speaking to Mr. Jones?" the ABC-coach heard herself ask.

"Yes, speaking." A dark, somewhat pleasant-to-listen-to voice sounded from the headphones the ABC-coach was wearing.

"Mr. Jones, you don't know me and we haven't met on any previous occasion. Nevertheless I'd like to ask you for two minutes of your time to explain the reason I am calling you. Is that okay?"

A silence ensued. It took the ABC-coach a gargantuan effort not to break it by babbling. However, she had been taught well by her mentors and coaches. She remembered a piece of advice she'd been given years ago, when she started off in sales. "Be comfortable in the silence that follows a closing question and respect the energy it radiates."

Five seconds passed. . .

It seemed like hours for the ABC-coach. She felt the anxiety take over, her palms started perspiring and she felt her armpits beginning to heat up. Nevertheless, she held her composure.

Finally, the voice replied, "Tell me how I can help."

"I am conducting interviews with successful leaders in sales, focusing specifically on their ways of creating performance of the sales team or teams they are leading. And I would like to learn from you how you lead your staff through this monster of a recession."

"Hah!" the voice exclaimed, "Recession, my behind." The ABC-coach thought she heard a short chuckle, albeit somewhat muffled by the background noise on the phone.

"Okay, tell me more," the voice continued.

"Well, ideally I'd like to interview you in several sessions to find out how and when you decided that a recession was not going to stop you from growing your revenue goals. I've checked your key figures online, and it baffled me that your company has had absolutely no hits from the latest economic woes."

"How many sessions?"

Mr. Jones found this young lady on the phone to be quite an interesting character. He had been interviewed before, but usually this entailed a very limited interview—in many instances, just one session. Here was someone who wanted to do a series of interviews.

"Well, ideally 25."

"Twenty-five?" Mr. Jones was a little taken aback by this. He figured about three interviews would be enough.

"Allow me to explain," the ABC-coach continued. "Mr. Jones, I understand that this might be a strange request. However, I don't think two or three interviews will give me the understanding I need and allow me to perform the best practices you and I will discuss."

"Go on. . ."

"Twenty-five ten-minute interviews on a weekly basis, resulting in 75 different actionable items."

"Okay, so it's just four hours of work in total. But why during a 25-week period?"

"That's easy. I want to immediately apply in practice what I have learned from you. And I want to create momentum by forcing myself into a weekly habit of taking action. I've learned a lot during my past interviews, which I did in a more traditional way, sometimes two or three hours at a time. But I didn't follow up on all my action items because I got information overflow. So I came up with the concept of doing 25 short interviews with a maximum of ten minutes per interview."

"Okay, so how about doing an interview for each letter of the alphabet, minus the A you got during this call?" Mr. Jones figured this might just be a little more fun than he imagined. This young lady clearly had some experience interviewing managers and high performers if she'd up with this idea. AND, she gave HIM the idea of following the alphabet. There clearly was some synergy here. . .

Now it was the ABC-coach's turn to think about the offer. She hadn't really made the connection with the alphabet yet. Twenty-five just seemed like a good number to her. Half a year's work with a week off for vacation, was her rationale.

Mister Jones continued:

"I agree to do the series, under three conditions:
   1. We work as a team: you learn from me but I also learn from you
   2. We apply Rule no. 5 whenever possible. Meaning we don't take ourselves so f***ing seriously
   3. My calendar rules: you miss an appointment, the fun is over."

"I can live with those rules," the ABC-coach said. "Mr. Jones, thank you for your time."

"No, no, thank you," Mr. Jones exclaimed. "This should be a very interesting and amusing way of mentoring someone. Talk to my assistant to schedule the appointments. Have a great day."

After the ABC-coach had set the dates for all of the 25 appointments, she dropped the receiver. She went through a score of different emotions, from anxiety about what was to come, to relief for having taken the step, apprehension about the conditions Mr. Jones had put forward, and elation for having had someone accept her concept.

She wondered about how it would all turn out and remembered that she would have to download a voice recording app on her Samsung. That would probably work a lot better. . .

She wrote three things in her brand new notebook:

1. Use a recording device

2. Remember Rule no. 5

3. Learn as if you would have to teach tomorrow what you have learned today

Building vs. Breaking

He who has not first laid his foundations may be able with great ability to lay them afterwards, but they will be laid with trouble to the architect and danger to the building.

~ Nicolo Macchiavelli

"Here's a contrast I have never really understood in the military. They break you down in boot camp just to build you up again after a few weeks of humiliation. I've always been interested in why drillmasters use that way of training—especially knowing that when these young men and women return home after having served, they lack the resilience to survive in normal society.

"It's an interesting discussion, though, one that has been going on for ages, it seems."

"But isn't the goal of the military to create leaders?" the ABC-coach wondered.

"Absolutely. How else can they fill their ranks with experienced NCOs and officers? The military improves skills to levels hardly found in the rest of society. Ask any Special Forces commando."

"So how does that translate to your day-to-day business, Mr. Jones?" the ABC-coach inquired. "I hardly see you as a drill sergeant in here."

"Of course you don't. Not my style. Though I can be pretty hot-headed sometimes," Mr. Jones grinned. "But people rarely see my angry side.

"The goal of building up a staff is to improve quality in your personnel, so you need to avoid using the stick-method and allow room for initiative, when appropriate," he continued. "Unfortunately, we forget to focus on these building blocks of a performance-driven staff. Incentives become givens instead of extra rewards, and we abandon our legacy for compromise."

"So what are the options to keep the building blocks in place?" the ABC-coach wanted to know.

"You have to understand you are the cement, first and foremost. You are what keeps the blocks together; you create the stability in your staff as a coach and a mentor; you allow the house to grow; you are responsible for the house being able to withstand shocks and tremors."

"So what you are saying is that if the quality of the cement is not sufficient, the house will crumble. Meaning that when you don't consciously and continuously pursue your own development, you risk that the cement you provide becomes weaker once the layers in your organization start stacking."

"Exactly!"

"So can you share the options you have to keep yourself performing at your highest level?"

"Of course a sort of success system comes in handy," Mr. Jones grinned. "Here's mine: read 60 minutes a day, listen to audiobooks in the car and regularly attend training seminars about subjects that pertain to your personal growth. I've been doing that for a little over 25 years. I have literally turned my car into a driving university, my study at home is filled with books, and I have visited virtually every entrepreneurial training system that the US has to offer. And I'm still learning!" Mr. Jones exclaimed.

"So tell me. . ." he continued. "What's yours?"

The ABC-coach had somewhat expected this question. She quickly said, "Modeling the best people in their profession, and writing down my impressions and goals daily."

"Hence the interview," Mr. Jones said. "Now I get it. Good idea. One day I might just model you for a specific trait. By the way, I'm very happy to see you use a recording app. So much easier to have a conversation."

"Oh, yes!" the ABC-coach added, "And I always listen to great advice and feedback. That's my third habit."

"Good, so you are continuously building your personality and breaking down barriers and paradigms," Mr. Jones smiled.

He extended his right hand, shook the ABC-coach's hand and said, "Congratulations, that's a great way to go about your personal growth. Don't worry about building or breaking; you'll do fine."

Mr. Jones escorted the ABC-coach out of his office and to the front door.

When the ABC-coach arrived home, she reflected on the fact that it felt as if she had had a huge breakthrough today. She wrote down in her notebook:

1. Everybody has a success system. Learn from them

2. Stones require cement. Be the cement

3. Be frank with people, and you will always know where you stand

larity vs. Confusion

I was to learn later that in life we tend to meet any new situation by reorganizing; and what a wonderful method it can be for creating the illusion of progress while producing confusion, inefficiency, and demoralization.

~ Petronius Arbiter

"Have you noticed how confusing working with other people in a business actually becomes when you start growing and are just not able to cope anymore with the influx of new situations that come with more customers?" Mr. Jones asked the ABC-coach as she came into the office.

"To be honest, I sometimes find it confusing just living with myself," she joked as she shook his hand.

"As do I," Mr. Jones said. "How can anyone expect us to be perfect at running an organization if we are still just learning how to stay on our feet? It seems only yesterday that I first set foot in this office, and I've been here more than twenty years. All that I have done in that time is just to create clarity in this confusion that is our business life."

"So what do you think obscures your view as a manager and performance coach in your company?" the ABC-coach inquired.

"Well, three things: politics, the number of performance indicators, and the different layers and how they are intertwined in an organization.

"You see, where there are people there is emotional energy. When this emotional energy is used for good, it drives us to maximum performance. But when it's used for the wrong reasons it turns against us in a flash. And then you get business politics. The trust cycle breaks down and people start to communicate differently: much more formally and with less frankness. When that happens, the discussion about performance gets more on edge, and we tend to want to create more control levers; thus we require more performance indicators. In order to monitor the extra number of levers, we need to build layers of management that allow us to simplify the information for the top layer.

"Stephen M.R. Covey wrote a very interesting book about the Speed of Trust, and just a few days ago something happened between two businessmen that seemed to underline his view that when trust is high not a lot of time needs to be lost. When Facebook took over Instagram a few days ago, it became clear that not a lot of confusion existed over the deal between the different shareholders. It was announced as being a solo-slim by the founder of Facebook, Steve Zuckerberg, and apparently the negotiation lasted as little as three days. Such a short process is rare for a billion-dollar deal."

"Also, the grapevine says that negotiation was strictly between both CEOs and did not involve too many other stakeholders. I find that interesting. Trust was high."

"So what are the options to increase clarity?" the ABC-coach asked.

"I'll just quote a few from the book and add my take if that's okay," Mr. Jones said. Picking up the book from behind his back, he began to read aloud.

"'In organizations a high level of trust is defined by a high level of collaboration and partnerships, unhindered communication, high transparency and strong belief that the staff is doing what is right.'"

"That's pretty idealistic, isn't it?" the ABC-coach asked.

"Well, I wouldn't say idealistic, I would call it a long-term objective," Mr. Jones smiled and went on.

"Options to improve this lie within the text itself: empower people to work together and partner up, have structured and open communication, and instill belief in your staff and your team.

"You can add sufficient qualification of new employees to that list as well, and training of new employees needs to be almost ruthless. You need to see how your new employees perform under high pressure to really assess their reactions. It has to do with how they see the world when the pressure goes up.

"Training needs to be a constant worry for a manager. Developing the staff to a level decided on early in the development process needs to be foremost on the manager's agenda, non-stop."

At that point in the interview the ABC-coach silently thanked herself for having the foresight to record the interviews instead of just jotting down what Mr. Jones had to say.

She shook his hand and left for home. When she got home she noticed that her neighbor Lucy had brought over a plate of lasagna verde. While she was eating, she opened her notebook for the third time and wrote down:

1. Have the best qualification system money can buy

2. Have transparent leadership skills

3. Gain trust through extreme levels of training

Debate vs. Delivery

Men of thought should have nothing to do with men of action.

~ Oscar Wilde

"What is the goal of debate?" Mr. Jones asked the ABC-coach. "Is it having the conversation, hitting a home run and presenting information in a way that enhances the process of reception of the information, or reflecting on how to proceed?

"The reality is that most meetings have an abysmal level of what I call blah-blah-isms and produce little or no actions and hardly any accountability.

"And to make matters worse, this is how we teach our young managerial staff that business should be run. We teach them how to use the words, practice the appropriate composure, and listen attentively. What we don't teach them is taking immediate daily action and follow-up.

"I mean, why do young kids like action heroes so much? Because they're lazy? No, because they dare to do things differently and because they are fearless.

"I'd love to have more action heroes on my staff - people who go out on a limb and enjoy the process. These people are indispensible. In fact, I attribute most of my success to a creed I received from one of my earliest mentors: 'One action a day.'"

It seemed that Mr. Jones ran a bit out of steam at the end of the sentence. A silence ensued.

Mr. Jones was clearly very emotional about this.

"You are pretty invested in this debate, aren't you?" the ABC-coach tried.

"What do you think?" Mr. Jones asked, smiling his biggest smile. "I get annoyed by the ridiculousness of mediocrity. Tons of meetings take place, but so few actually yield any results.

"That's why I like Jack Welch so much. Much can be said about this somewhat controversial top CEO, but I love the fact that he just asked the question 'What is the reality here?' continuously. It showed his involvement on all levels. Few top managers actually do that, and then most of the people who surround them deliver anything but partly fabricated numbers."

"But what are the options when reality seems so dire?"

"There is no arguing with a manager demanding timely results by a certain deadline. When the need is pressing, most people tend to deliver more than expected.

"Have a good project-follow-up system; know who does what by when by having a delegated task folder. I'll talk about those in detail in another interview," Mr. Jones added.

"Any other ideas?" the ABC-coach wanted to know.

"Stand above the debate. And if you feel you are getting sucked in, create distance from the workplace. Find a way, walk around, inspect the warehouse. It doesn't really matter what you do, just do it quickly."

"So you're saying you're pretty much against debates and for deliveries," the ABC-coach continued.

"Well, no. I'm all for an open debate. I just feel I need to control when the debate ends and actions get taken in my staff. Everybody has a say and can question my decisions, but when the decision has been made we execute and stay on course until the information flowing in proves that the course might be right according to the compass, but the direction is leading us away from our destination – say, into a storm.

"That's when the reflection comes in, as well as experience."

"And wisdom," the ABC-coach added.

"And knowing that it doesn't matter WHO's right, only what's right and WHEN it is right."

The ABC-coach felt she had had a really intense few minutes and decided to cut the interview short. It seemed that she had stepped on a sensitive topic, and she didn't want to bother Mr. Jones any more, as he had given her a run for her money already.

When she arrived home, she picked up her notebook and wrote down:

1. Have staff deliver more, discuss less

2. Create distance from the emotional aspect of the debate

3. Know the difference between course and direction

Example vs. Earthly

Earthly minds, like mud walls, resist the strongest batteries; and though, perhaps, sometimes the force of a clear argument may make some impression, yet they nevertheless stand firm, keep out the enemy, truth, that would captivate or disturb them.

~ John Locke

"What does your ideal manager look like?" Mr. Jones looked inquiringly at the ABC-coach, wondering what she was going to say. He figured that by now she might have some idea how she would want to lead, based on her own life experience and the subjects they had already covered during past interviews. He was really interested in seeing her role models blend into one idea—knowing full well he'd probably be in there as well.

He smiled to himself, thinking of his modeling time, when he was still awed by so many top managers, before he realized they, too, were human after all, with human needs and flaws much like his own.

He always felt humbled and honored when people like the ABC-coach came to him for a model of a business leader, no matter how many times he'd already been involved in a similar project.

"Well, let me think about it," the ABC-coach said. Looking around the room as she thought, she noticed the painting of a beautiful race horse on the wall on her left side. The horse was pitch black, its head stretching forward toward the finish line, with its mane in the wind and the jockey bent over its outstretched neck with a determined grin on his face.

She decided to focus on the jockey to collect her thoughts. She wondered what kind of traits a good jockey would need in order to get a horse to move that fast.

"Well, I'd like my team leader to be dynamic, confident and able to get results." She figured winning the race would be the same as getting the desired business result.

"Nicely put. Did you notice the painting on my left side?" Mr. Jones remarked casually, smiling at her.

The ABC-coach blushed a bit. Was she that obvious?

"Trust me, most people who come in here look at the picture at some point. Honestly, looking at that picture gives me peace and makes me realize that I'm a jockey myself, albeit from my desk," Mr. Jones smiled.

"But isn't the reality that most managers have an image of being more of a desk jockey?"

"Quite true," said Mr. Jones. "Because of the bureaucracy model left over from the industrial age, managers often feel handicapped and feel that their horse—their business—isn't running an optimal race."

"So what can we do to get our business to perform optimally?"

"First we have to realize which paradigms are left over in our brains from the industrial age. It is peculiar that most politicians, unions and media alike are so stuck in the same story, tirelessly trying to hold back ideas like diversification or new business practices by over-regulating certain areas. You and I have been brought up under the paradigm of going to school, building a so-called nuclear family, having the same job for our entire life, and then ending up with a pension, enjoying Medicare or a facsimile of that in other countries. We have to realize that our team dynamics will be undergoing constant changes, and so will the people on the staff."

"So how can you change the idea that your staff is like a nuclear family—always staying together?" The ABC-coach leaned forward as she related to what Mr. Jones said about team, staff and family. In her opinion, her staff was and had always been part of her family, sometimes even more than her own family, far away in Ireland.

"Simple trick: just realize that families come in many different forms nowadays, single parents re-marrying, single parents raising children, young marrying old and older, kids staying home until they're thirty. The same is happening to the homogeneity of the staff. People come and go, and some core people stay because their values are so aligned with the leader that it is just out of the question that they leave the family.

"And this is but one example. Many paradigms rule our thought patterns and have absolutely no more value in our lives than they do in our business. So the question then becomes: are you going to be the *pater familias* that resists change and alienates people, or the one open to change in all forms, showing respect for values and people and being able to help others? It's no longer about just hiring and firing; it's becoming more about your staff as a family."

"So what options do we have to be an example for our staff?"

"Determine your values, live by them and show them to others."

"I know that part," the ABC-coach said. "One of my first mentors gave me a list of values and had me just strike out those that didn't feel like they belonged with me. When I had twenty left, he gave me the assignment of synthesizing two values into one until I had five left. I have come to live along the lines of those personal values. Later on I did the same exercise for my business, with the same result."

"Nice. And did you share your values with others?"

"Yes, and since then I have seen lots of changes around me. People that I have known for years have become inspired or scared by the changes—in the latter case they mostly just disappeared from my radar. Strangely enough, I still stay on theirs, though." She smiled at this thought, because she realized that social media had had a huge influence on her following in her business.

She suddenly realized Mr. Jones had just turned the tables on her, asking her questions she should have been asking. Nevertheless, having this conversation was pleasant enough as it was, so she decided to leave her line of questioning for time being.

Mr. Jones continued, "And do you regularly check back on your values to see if you're still aligned?"

"Yes, during my weekly review time I always take five minutes to ask myself the question, 'Did I live up to these values every day of the last week?' Then I ask myself, 'Am I being too critical here? Or not critical enough?' I always write the answer in my journal."

Mr. Jones smiled. "So you keep it down to earth?"

"Yes. It works for me, and that's all that matters."

"Then you're the example and I'm just an old fart." His eyes brightened, the wrinkles around his eyes started pointing upward, his nose twitched and the corners of this mouth raised up. He let out a bellowing laugh.

After a minute he stopped laughing and looked at the ABC-coach. "Just keep on doing what you're doing now and you'll be fine."

The ABC-coach got up from her comfortable chair, shook Mr. Jones' hand and left the office, wondering who was outperforming whom now.

When she got home, she poured herself a nice glass of Chardonnay 2008, enjoying the aroma of pear, tropical fruit and melon while writing in her spiral notebook:

1. Define, live by and review your values regularly

2. Keep a journal of your progress

3. A staff is NOT a nuclear family

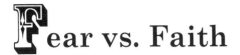ear vs. Faith

*A true friend knows your weaknesses but shows you
your strengths; feels your fears but fortifies your faith;
sees your anxieties but frees your spirit; recognizes your
disabilities but emphasizes your possibilities.*

~ William Arthur Ward

"What drives us forward in business? Is it the fear of
being overrun by our competitors or the absolute faith
that we are doing what we are meant to be doing?" Mr.
Jones asked.

"Interesting question. I think without fear my job
wouldn't even exist. People need coaches to help them
deal with their paradigms and assist them in moving
forward, because the pain of staying behind is larger
than the pain of moving forward."

"Precisely. As long as people have fears, we will have
employees." Mr. Jones looked at the ABC-coach very
seriously, understanding that having stated this truth,
some explanation and nuancing would be required.

"A coach's goal is to create mental toughness that allows for a total elimination of fears, an avoidance of falling back into old habits.

"Moving forward in faith is a talent few possess and many aspire to have.

"When I was just starting as a manager, our staff did a very interesting exercise. It was loosely based on the computer game 'Lemmings.'"

"I remember that game. You had to lead a cute little furry animal pack through an obstacle course. The pack usually followed the leader, even if you made a stupid mistake. So if the leader chose poorly, everybody suffered."

"Only in our real-life simulation, the leader was in the back, and he was the only one not blindfolded. Even the person in front was blindfolded. The leader then had to signal by means of body language if the head of the group had to go left, right, back or forward and to what degree. We had to walk around trees, avoid bushes and stay on our feet.

"Afterward, we were all questioned and it turned out that the people who immediately admitted they were the most comfortable were always the people in the center. The person in front felt less at ease physically, and the person giving the direction felt more mental stress and worry because he wanted to save his colleagues in front from bouncing against a tree. In some people this fear even caused a breakdown in communication.

"One of the main tasks I occupy myself with in this organization consists of nothing but getting people to understand that carrot-and-stick is old-school and rarely works on the younger generation. My biggest worry is that young people have so little fear that they don't see the fine line between stupidity and bravery anymore." Mr. Jones sighed and looked at his nicely manicured hands.

"So what are the options to work with those situations?"

"First, give feedback in a rational manner. Understand that it's just business and that it is your role to maintain a business composure. Help people when necessary to go from 'Oh, S**t' to 'Yes!'

"Mark Goulston wrote a marvelous little book about that where he describes how our reptilian brain hijacks us sometimes so we go into complete idiocy and turn into rambling dumbos. He also shows a very simple mind trick we can perform to go back to our normal selves most of the time Here's the trick:

1. 'Oh, s**t.' Acknowledge you're panicking, and if you can, don't talk to anyone.

2. 'Oh, God.' Breathe through your nose and let go.

3. 'Oh, Jeez.' Repeat phase 1, 2 and 3 as long as needed.

4. 'Oh, well.' Get moving; start thinking about actions you can take, but don't take them (yet).

5. 'O.K.' Do what you need to do."

"Any other options to help people go through their fears?"

"Yes, put them in your position. I sometimes place people in my seat and then ask them for advice on a situation I have with an employee. When it is really a good employee that is going through a difficult patch, I'm even capable of putting the employee himself in my place and ask him what I would do.

"This has a few advantages: the employee feels heard, the employee is giving feedback to himself, and I get less tired," Mr. Jones grinned. "Now of course, this is challenging for me as well, as usually the employee always wants to explain him- or herself, but that is not the goal. The goal is to eliminate the fear the employee is feeling and to help him help himself, starting from a helicopter view."

"I love that idea," the ABC-coach told Mr. Jones. "It helps empower employees and gives them the tools to overcome any fear they might have of being hit with a stick."

"Exactly. Many an employee saved himself from dismissal by applying this method."

The ABC-coach shook Mr. Jones' hand and left for home. She thought about the last point Mr. Jones had explained, and concluded that using empathy this way made of lot of sense.

She returned home and wrote in her spiral notebook:

1. In the front end or the back end of the organization the intensity of emotions is always higher

2. Putting an employee in the manager's seat helps provide valuable feedback for both parties

3. Disarm situations by going from 'Oh, s**t' to 'Yes!'

Gadget vs. Gainful

We make our gadgets our own by the way that we use them, with or without the permission of the manufacturer.

– Laura Moncur

"Why do we use gadgets in our business lives?"

"Well, I suppose they make life easier, make us more efficient and allow us to preserve our energy," the ABC-coach answered. "At least it's the goal of the advertising and marketing department to convince us of that."

"You hit it on the head—especially that last part. Gadgets are getting more and more elaborate as our society grows and expands into more complex, multilayered structures. We cannot live without our Blackberries and iPads anymore. But the question remains: what percentage of our gadgets do we actually use and are useful for our lives?"

"Well, I suppose we can sell any new habit to ourselves. It doesn't matter if the habit helps us or hurts us," the ABC-coach mused, thinking about the smoking habit she'd broken a few years earlier.

"I am a fervent believer in streamlining new technology in a company. Sometimes you can get more value from a ten dollar white paper on project management than from a fully-grown software package costing several thousands."

"So what system do you use?" the ABC-coach wanted to know.

"I use a very simple model for managing my projects and following them up. A white paper I acquired from David Allen described a very easy way to transform my Outlook into a great follow-up tool. My e-mails are sorted into Actionable Items, Reviewable Items, Delegated Items, and a tickler file. My projects are managed through my Outlook Tasks, and the actions connected to these projects have separate categories.

"It took me about one hour to implement, four hours to sort through my different tasks and assign them to the categories, and two hours per week to review them. It works wonderfully!"

"But what is the secret, then?"

"Applying it with rigorous focus.

"The reality is that most tech businesses are built on offering too much, with too little tutoring and tech support to use their software. We are given a manual, and that will have to do."

"So how can we determine when a gadget is useful for us and worth adding to our toolkit?"

"Clear and simple: ask yourself if it works for you *and* for your employees, how fast you can implement it, and only then ask how much it costs.

"Yes, we need gadgets. Yes, we need new technology, and new applications can improve your business performance on a daily basis. But do they fit the system you are running?

"Working with key performance indicators, I came across a very interesting business model called BSC Designer. The great thing about this particular system is not that the designers invented something brand new, but rather that they created something that is actually layered in such a way that small companies as well as large corporations are able to use the system at their respective price points. You can basically build or re-engineer your own KPI structure in less than a day, going through all the different aspects of your business. And the great thing is that it's free for all, unless you want to expand your options to include a quick solution for getting even more ways of analyzing new information from the system."

"But how do they make their money if it is free?"

"They offer support through online videos. Sometimes for free, sometimes paid. They can re-purpose those videos as much as they want, so the information they send keeps its value even after a while."

"So understanding how a business model works is as important as understanding the technology itself." The ABC-coach began to understand a little bit of Mr. Jones's philosophy.

"Right, so in purchasing even the smallest items some due diligence is required."

Mr. Jones looked at the books behind him. "Here's an interesting book that describes patterns in business. It's called *Free: The Future of a Radical Price*. This is what Amazon writes about the book: '*Free* makes the compelling case that in many instances businesses can profit more from giving things away than they can by charging for them. Far more than a promotional gimmick, Free is a business strategy that may well be essential to a company's survival.'

"So understanding how 'Free' works will change your business perspective overnight!"

Thanking Mr. Jones for this insight, the ABC-coach left the building. She remembered looking at many of the websites of her colleagues and realized in a flash that almost ALL of them were giving away free information ALL the time. She wondered if they weren't giving away too much, instead of creating more value.

When she got home, she wrote three things in her spiral notebook:

1. Don't look at gadgets; look at how useful an item is for YOU

2. Understanding FREE is building a solid business strategy

3. Organize e-mail in actionable, reviewable, delegated and tickler items

Habits vs. Hades

Habits are like supervisors that you don't notice.

– Hannes Messemer

The ABC-coach was getting used to the idea of spending no more than ten minutes at a time in Mr. Jones' office. In the beginning she had felt as if it were not enough, she had so many questions. Having gone through several interviews, however, she now felt she got the tempo, and the rate at which she was changing her ways of handling and looking at things was changing rapidly.

He always started with a simple kickoff. After proceeding to discuss the goals of his actions, he continued to the reality of what was going on with other businesses. Then the question, "What are our options?" was answered by giving three simple ideas. This system resembled some of the coaching methods that the ABC-coach had previously seen in books by professional coaches.

Upon entering the office she smiled at Mr. Jones and said, "It's becoming a habit, isn't it?"

"What do you mean?" Mr. Jones wanted to know.

"Well, coming here, spending about ten minutes with you and then going home and acting on what you've been teaching me."

"Isn't it great?" Mr. Jones chuckled. "It's probably somewhat different from the first few interviews we did. It seemed you were struggling with the methodology."

"That's right," the ABC-coach agreed. "Probably because it wasn't a habit yet."

"Yes, it takes about eight to ten weeks to really get the mechanics of any new mental habit. For most people coming from the industrial age, that proves to be quite a challenge because they were used to repetitive work all their lives. I listened to an audiobook by Brian Tracy once from the nineties, and he talked about a study on how fast our society moves. Calculations, he told us, have indicated that we will have an increase in knowledge, technology, transactions, relationships, and in society by a factor as big as what we had to endure in the last 2,000 years by the end of the 21st century. That means we will have to go through as many changes in the next century as humanity went through in the 2,000 years before us."

"Wow, that must be hell for some people."

"I have to admit that sometimes I feel like I'm going through Hades myself. It's hard to keep up," Mr. Jones admitted.

"The reality is that we cannot turn back the clock. All politics aside, we will move forward faster and faster, and people resisting change will have a harder and harder time staying in touch. There is not only a financial gap but also a knowledge gap."

"So what are our options?" The ABC-coach knew what was expected of her.

"Our goal as business leaders and managers should be to empower people to embrace change, not resist it. We need to learn to build a management structure that will be set loose from the industrial business model, meaning that change needs to become a habitual thing. People will need to let go of some of the old beliefs that they brought with them from their formative years.

"Our task is to create sustainable models and choose our performance indicators based more on change and less on end-of-the-day business numbers. You might call me an idealist, but I firmly believe that most so-called gurus do not go far enough in their attitude toward change. They give us applicable, simple ideas, but not what managers really need: a best-practices model based on the new knowledge society instead of industrial society.

"A second thing we really need to understand is that to embrace change we need to become comfortable at being uncomfortable. We need to be focused on taking at least one daily action that instills change in our beings and our businesses. And no, I don't mean an action list. I mean asking yourself the question in the morning: 'What can I do to be the change I want to see in my business and my life?' This question has been driving me forward in my life and keeps me on my toes.

"Studying the future is also a very valuable concept."

Mr. Jones reached behind him to pick up a book labeled *Revolutionary Wealth*. The right top corner of the multi-colored cover had been torn off. The author's names were typed in pale blue, the title was bright red, and behind the letters was a mandala-like circle.

"I've read every book by Alvin Toffler and his wife Heidi. Even though they were very wrong in some areas, as futurists inevitably are at times, I found them prescient in spotting the patterns that drive our society before these patterns were manifested."

"So what you are saying is that it's not necessarily about doing what gurus say and write, but having the conversation about what ideas they bring to the world."

"That's right!"

The ABC-coach shook Mr. Jones's hand and left for home. She logged on to Amazon and started looking at books about the future. Then she sat down with her spiral notebook and wrote down three things she would work on this week:

1. Focus on learning more about how to manage in a knowledge society

2. Ask yourself daily: "What can I do to be the change I want to see?"

3. Take one action daily based on the answer to action 2

Impulsiveness vs. Indiscriminateness

*Small opportunities are often the beginning
of great enterprises.*

– Demosthenes

"Here's an idea! Why don't we go out into the company and I'll introduce you to our most creative employee," Mr. Jones said.

As they walked out into the corridor, which was filled with huge pictures coming straight from a comic book, she noticed a small sign written in blue capital letters: "If you're not impulsive sometimes, you're not creative anymore."

Isn't that interesting, she thought. She had always believed that being impulsive and just blurting out whatever it was you wanted to say was career suicide.

"Interesting sign," she said. "Do you encourage impulsiveness in your company?"

"Well, yes and no," Mr. Jones explained. "As a manager, I hate it when people start working too far outside of the box. It just creates more paperwork and thus more liability. In the words of Peter Drucker, 'Most of what we call management consists of making it difficult for people to get their work done.'

"Impulsiveness has had a bad rap in the industrial society, where we had a pre-determined life path to follow and drawing inside the lines was mostly a prerequisite for some social mobility," Mr. Jones explained. "I give my people a certain amount of freedom to follow their impulses and their ideas, as long as it doesn't interfere with their current workload."

"But, knowing how much a knowledge worker costs, doesn't that immediately put a lot of pressure on your cashflow and your productivity?"

"That depends on how you define productivity. In the old days, we used to think about productivity as merely an addition of efficiency (doing things right) and effectiveness (doing the right things), or a derivative of those concepts. In the knowledge worker age, that definition has been receiving more and more pressure. On the one hand, you need to report on your progress—that's a no-brainer, right? But then again, you need to constantly come up with new ideas. How can you do that without some form of freedom to be impulsive and to break patterns?

"The reality is that most companies think that coming up with new ideas is a once-a-year standalone project that requires no real follow-up by a specific project staff and is just a prerequisite to keep some appearance of democracy for their employees."

"But you disagree, I take it?" the ABC-coach inquired.

"Absolutely I do."

Meanwhile they arrived at the production facility, where they were met by the head of production.

"It is a pleasure to meet you, ma'am. I've heard a lot about you. I'm Jack."

"So," Mr. Jones smiled, "I'll leave you two to talk. I'll be on the floor. Talk to you later."

Mr. Jones walked to the other side of the production facility, wearing his white helmet and waving to everyone he passed by.

"You must really like working for him," the ABC-coach told Jack.

"Absolutely! He saved me from becoming a really dull blue collar employee."

"How do you mean?"

"Well, I've always had this gift of putting two and two together, so to speak. So whenever two ideas were brought to me, I could make them into a new concept altogether. I never realized how special it was, because it all came naturally to me. I just used it indiscriminately. Whenever I had an idea I'd run with it. Now I have this simple PDA that allows me to write down my ideas whenever I need to write them, and I bring them to Mr. Jones. He looks at them and we work out a plan to get them done. I once thought of a way to combine Magic cards with a gaming console by using digital scanning methods.

"He promoted me to project leader overnight, and even though this specific idea did not turn out to be the greatest invention on earth, it still was good enough for the gaming community out there."

Jack grinned at this, showing his tattoo of *World of Warcraft* on his left wrist. "I could have been content just gaming until the end of my days, but now I have a purpose: finding new ideas to create synergies between gaming and real life. People used to call me impulsive, but now I know better."

"What options do you believe Mr. Jones uses to create more impulsiveness in his business?" the ABC-coach wondered.

"Well, keep taking gutsy decisions once in a while. Also, only hire people that are multifunctional AND enthusiastic."

"Like you, you mean," the ABC-coach said.

"Yeah, like me. I love what I do and I have full control of who joins my staff. No recruitment happens without me being involved. I want to be able to only work with creative people."

The ABC-coach shook Jack's hand, went home, sat down and wrote down three ideas in her notebook:

1. Never underestimate the potential of your staff

2. Impulsiveness is not the same as being indiscriminate; there is method to the madness

3. Ask Jack out

Jack-in-the-office vs. Jockey

Most managers were trained to be the thing they most despise - bureaucrats.

~ Alvin Toffler

"What is the primary goal of management?" Mr. Jones asked the ABC-coach.

"Well, let me think," the ABC-coach said. She looked again at the painting of the beautiful race horse on the wall on her left side. She wondered what kind of traits a good jockey would need in order to get a horse to move that fast but came up with no immediate answer.

"I couldn't say," the ABC-coach replied.

"It's winning the game with honor. Isn't that amazing? I look at this picture every day, imagining being the owner and trainer of this horse. You've done everything right. You've groomed the horse, had a team manage its health on a daily basis. You were sure that you did everything right, and yet here you are, in second place."

"You mean to say this picture was taken before the finish. Ouch, that must have hurt," the ABC-coach said.

"How do you come back from a knock like that? Your horse is still fine. It will most likely run and win the next big race.

"Unfortunately, the reality is that perception dictates that you've lost. Fingers will be pointed at you and your team, and heads are most likely going to roll. In a business environment your mail server will likely not be able to handle the deluge of e-mails that will be coming in from all directions asking for an explanation of the loss, while your reality says you've done your utmost.

"Forces will be dragging you toward analysis paralysis, where you get lost in the myriads of performance indicators that your horse has been measured upon—which only reinforces your already shaky mental state."

"You'll start to feel depressed, not because you've lost, but because of the fallout. Trust me, the feeling of loss goes away fairly quickly when you pick up your next win, but the fallout stays. You might end up having to answer questions about that one loss three years running."

"But how do you deal with loss?" the ABC-coach asked. "I guess it's about mental toughness, right? I'd call it mental dynamism, based on your belief system telling you that you are on the right track."

"Too right," Mr. Jones smiled. "Here's the thing: I'm not a horse whisperer, but I believe that the horse in second place suffers more from the jockey and its caretakers being depressed than from coming in second place. And it's the same with business. Your performance system suffers more from the emotions behind the results than from the results themselves.

"The reality is that bureaucracy is not a solution for a crisis. It never was and it never will be. Overanalysis will keep the horse out of the next race, and the next, and the next."

"So what are the options for avoiding 'analysis paralysis' in a crisis?"

"Go out and listen to people. Move the vehicle forward—or backward—but move it.

"Get the staff aligned behind the next ·goal and go for it. Then track on a weekly basis how everything is going until the forward momentum that brought you so close to that first place comes back. Because, trust me, it will be gone for a while. How long, that's for you as a manager to decide.

"Do you know the difference between a bureaucrat and a leader?" Mr. Jones asked the ABC-coach.

"Tell me. You seem to be on a roll," the ABC-coach smiled.

"Here's something a top manager told me at the beginning of my career: take the bureaucrat out of a business manager and you have a good leader, with vision, maybe even mission and values that will continue to move the ship out of the storm. Take the leader out of the business manager and you have a bureaucrat that will run your ship aground.

"I will talk in detail about crisis management later on, but you see that in a crisis you want a captain at the helm and not the administrative assistant."

The ABC-coach returned home, thinking about how strongly Mr. Jones rejected the need for more administration in his own company.

She opened her notebook and wrote down three points:

1. Refuse to go into analysis paralysis, no matter what

2. Align the staff toward the next goal

3. Have weekly follow-up meetings during a crisis

Koffee klatsch vs. Kickoff

This coffee plunges into the stomach. . . the mind is aroused, and ideas pour forth like the battalions of the Grand Army on the field of battle. . . Memories charge at full gallop. . . the light cavalry of comparisons deploys itself magnificently; the artillery of logic hurry in with their train of ammunition; flashes of wit pop up like sharp-shooters.

– Honoré de Balzac

"Why do people engage in new activities? Why do businesses organize these well-intentioned kickoff events when a new project is started? Why don't we just start? What kind of psychology are we using when we organize parties BEFORE any results are met? Don't you find it odd that companies spend so much money on what seems to be a useless exercise of imputed significance, exuberance, and sometimes even decadence?"

Apparently Mr. Jones wasn't too fond of big events in any kind of organization, the ABC-coach thought.

"Personally, I couldn't care less what people do with their money, as long as results are being achieved and the people are happy," he continued. "The thing is that most of the events I have attended seemed more like a koffee klatsch, where people exchanged pleasantries but with hardly any real result to show."

Mr. Jones continued, "Actually, the kickoff in most sports games is about the least spectacular event of the entire game—except on those rare occasions when one of the teams gets to score really quickly after that.

"That should be your aim during a kickoff meeting: how can we score a quick win in the least possible time? And trust me, most quick wins are created over koffee klatsches," Mr. Jones smiled.

"Oh, so you mean that the real kickoff in business lies in the networking done during those kickoff events," the ABC-coach concluded.

"Just so. In a later interview I'll elaborate on the choices between small events and big events, but for now the reality of the matter is that any event is just an event if the participants don't bring their A-game."

"What do you mean, exactly?" the ABC-coach asked.

"Well, what are the participants' goals? See, you don't convince people to make crazy changes just like that—unless you're Tony Robbins, of course. Imagine they come with an attitude of 'I wonder whether this elephant is going to turn out to be a mouse again,' instead of 'Great, let's see how we can use this. What's the one thing I'll be taking to the office from this?' What's going to be the difference in results?"

"So the reality is. . ." The ABC-coach waved her hands invitingly to Mr. Jones, as if to let him fill in the blank.

"The reality is that drinking coffee during a kickoff event is essential for your company's success and your personal success."

"And what are the options you would suggest?"

"You can read a gazillion books on networking. And the thing is that they are all right. Every technique works when used appropriately. But here's what it boils down to: why don't you start acting as if you are the host? What would you do differently if you were the host of the event? How would you talk to people differently? What actions would you take? How do you create goodwill for your goals?"

"So what you are saying is to organize your own party?"

"If you play an instrument, go for it," Mr. Jones smiled. "Nobody can resist a musician's charm."

The ABC-coach was a little confused, because it seemed to be a long way from the events and stiff-upper-lipness she had met in her years as a manager.

"On the other hand, be dead serious on the business issues. State clearly what you stand for and stand firm," Mr. Jones said. "A lot of politics is played during that kind of event, with most people unaware of what the stakes are.

"So learn to say, 'Let's discuss this over coffee,'" Mr. Jones concluded.

The ABC-coach thanked Mr. Jones for his insight and left the office. Upon leaving the office she noticed for the first time how close the coffee machine actually was to Mr. Jones' office.

Now isn't that interesting, the ABC-coach thought. It occurred to her that Mr. Jones, whose office door was always open, probably knew more about the scuttlebutt in his company because he was closer to the coffee machine, where informal meetings typically take place.

When she came home, she laughed out loud, realizing she had run out of coffee.

She went to her neighbors, a nice couple with two kids and a dog, and rang the bell.

"Hi. Can I trouble you for some coffee? I'm out," she asked Joan, a petite but extremely energetic mother of three young kids with a beautician practice at home.

"Sure, come on in. I just made a fresh pot. Would you like some?" Joan smiled invitingly.

The ABC-coach didn't know how she could refuse. She realized that coffee opens doors in every direction.

When she came back after a nice chat, she took out her notebook and wrote down:

1. Practice the 6 Ps before an event (Proper Prior Planning Prevents Poor Performance)

2. Act as if you're the host during the event

3. Invite people you want to connect with for coffee between sessions

Lofty vs. Low-profile

He was a scholar, and a ripe and good one,
Exceedingly wise, fair-spoken and persuading,
Lofty and sour to those that loved him not,
But to those men that sought him sweet as summer.

~ William Shakespeare

"Have you ever had the opportunity to see a really lofty plan fail?" Mr. Jones asked.

"Multinationals do this all the time. They take a lot of time thinking about what the ideal outcome is and work out a plan to implement changes in measurement on all levels. They find consultants to support the process, who then become amazed at how different the reality is compared to the perception senior management may appear to have had beforehand.

"I'm choosing my words carefully, because senior management realizes that there is a gap—it's inevitable in such a large organization. They just don't realize how big a gap there is.

"Lower-profile projects—with a lot less budget—sometimes achieve bigger results because they are able to switch gears a lot faster," Mr. Jones said.

"But don't the same principles apply to small and large projects alike?" the ABC-coach asked. "I mean, it's all about planning, doing, checking, and reacting, right?"

"Absolutely!" Mr. Jones exclaimed. "The main reason we deviate from that process is the human interaction it requires. We are not automatons. Ultimately, emotions drive our decisions, not numbers. Numbers create emotions, nothing more.

"The reality is that lofty and low-profile are complementary. Momentum comes from grand decisions and small decisions alike. I will go into more detail when we have the discussion about quantity or quality.

"There is no inside track to performance success. It requires time and energy invested in the right things at the right time."

"So what are our options?" the ABC -coach wanted to know. Since she fully understood what Mr. Jones was saying, she decided not to take too much of his time elaborating.

"Not so fast," Mr. Jones said, smiling. "Don't you want to know how and when we are motivated to choose the size and scope of projects?"

"Budget, I guess," the ABC-coach replied.

"And ego," Mr. Jones completed. "No, seriously, it has to do with impatience and perception. The more impatient you become with the lack of forward momentum, the further you want to jump. And that's when you start spending money in amounts that won't justify the change. And perception: how about this? We get everyone in the same room for one big event and announce huge changes, then we go back to our offices and the change only comes in two years. What would you say as an employee?"

"So what you are saying, Mr. Jones, is that impatience and perception make us choose between lofty projects and the low profile approach."

"Hence, the principle remains the same," the ABC-coach continued. "We organize a project; we reflect on the past, present, and future steps; and act according to our analyses; because it's the best we can do."

The ABC-coach thanked Mr. Jones for his time.

While she was driving home, she remembered one of her old bosses, on his last day with the company she worked with, saying, "Be patient, your time will come. Take big steps in small numbers or small steps in big numbers. Either will move you toward your goal and result."

When she arrived home, she was welcomed by her cat Spiffy. The ginger tomcat had been her companion during the last ten years of her career. Smiling down at her furry friend, she said, "You're probably one of the few creatures in the world who saw me do all these crazy things, aren't you?"

The cat looked at her knowingly, his tail high up in the air, purring out his pleasure at the attention he was receiving from her.

It struck her, now that they were almost halfway through the alphabet, that the simplicity of what Mr. Jones thought, said, and did stood in stark contrast to his vast knowledge about business and life. Yet it seemed as if all the analysis in the world wasn't enough for him to predict success.

Mr. Jones didn't care about how something looked; he cared about what worked, no matter what the context was and no matter what lofty ideas were behind it. He was organized, yet disorganized as well, leaving room for creativity. He was straight talking, yet always nuanced his ideas in a disarming manner. He was fun and serious.

She was interested in what he would have to say about the other letters in the alphabet and what surprises were still in store for her.

Eventually Spiffy jumped off her lap, and she picked up her notebook. She wrote down three action points:

1. Plan, Do, Check, React—no matter what

2. Forget about the look and feel of the project; it's what the project focuses on that counts

3. The ability to switch gears faster is the key to business success

Misery vs. Mastermind

He that teaches himself, has a fool for a master

~ Unknown

"I want to introduce you to some people I work closely with," Mr. Jones said to the ABC-coach.

He rose from his desk and said, "Put on your coat; it's cold outside."

As the ABC-coach picked up her coat, she asked, "Where are we going?"

"I want to introduce you to some of the people that saved my behind more than once in the last twenty years."

Mr. Jones escorted the ABC-coach to his car, a red Mustang convertible. The sun was shining brightly today, and it seemed the car only grew in size because of it. The leather seats and chrome on the door made her admire Mr. Jones's taste for what is beautiful in the world even more.

"One of the few benefits I tend to enjoy nowadays," he said, smiling. "I'll turn it in next week and get back to my Prius."

The ABC-coach would not have believed Mr. Jones to be into that kind of status symbol, but nevertheless, once she sat in the leather passenger seat, she understood how this was vastly different from her own Volkswagen Rabbit.

While they were driving, Mr. Jones explained where they were going. "I have a weekly get-together with some of my oldest friends. We change venues weekly, opening our houses to each other in sequence. This week it's my turn.

"I want to show you what changed me into the person I am today, and I need you to meet my team for that— not my staff, but my team," he added.

"Is there a difference for you?" the ABC-coach asked.

"Absolutely! My team has been with me ever since I started to get serious about personal development. My staff has changed members so many times it's hard to count.

"See, you don't bring your challenges to your staff, necessarily; you bring them to your team."

"And who can I expect to be on your team?" the ABC-coach asked.

"This team consists of people like me, with functions similar to mine, who have a family and, above all else, have the guts to stand up to me and say that I'm wrong."

"And what's the value of those meetings?"

"To be honest, immeasurable in KPIs, but so valuable you cannot even imagine. I used to turn inside myself when I was in a bad place mentally. I felt it hard to share that with my staff at work, with my family, or with my friends. So the misery started to devour me.

"Then one of my oldest and dearest friends said that I should come to his mastermind group. I hadn't heard about anything like that, but I was desperate and so I joined. The group welcomed me, but I was pretty intimidated by these men and women. They seemed to be very knowing about worldly matters."

Mr. Jones swerved the car into his driveway, and the ABC-coach was immediately struck by the simplicity of his home. This was not a Hollywood house, nor was it a castle. Granted, the garden was perfectly maintained and the driveway was clean as a whistle.

They drove up to the side of the house, passing the white brick building on the left. Behind the house, a beautiful hazelnut tree accentuated the garden and created restful shade. Mr. Jones parked the car just in front of the garage, which was separate from the house and about fifteen yards from the back door.

"Do you like it?" Mr. Jones seemed a little uncertain at this point. He knew his house was probably not what the ABC-coach was expecting. Nor, as a matter of fact, what most people expected when they first saw it. It was a beautiful old house with a large porch which covered the entire back of the house. The ABC-coach felt it resonated in a way with how Mr. Jones actually talked and moved.

"I do," she said, and she meant it. It made perfect sense.

"So how do you build such a group of people around you?" she asked while they walked the path to the back door.

"Find and surround yourself with positive people. Have faith in the synergy between the different people in your mastermind group. And share your challenges as much as you would share your successes.

"Now, let me introduce you to some of my friends. . ." Mr. Jones said, as he opened the back door and they entered his home.

The ABC-coach returned home two hours later, her head filled with new ideas as well as old ones that had come back after lying dormant, sometimes for a very long time.

She wrote down three action items in her notebook:

1. Find and surround yourself with positive people

2. Be open to input at all times

3. Build a team outside your staff

Never again vs. Now what?

"So what? Now what?"

~ Loral Langemeier

"In 1929 most politicians and economists—though not realizing the severity of the crisis ahead of them—vowed never again to let the economy be at the mercy of too much emotion. Stability was key, and the discussion turned from accepting recessions as basically a good thing to ways of achieving stability."

The ABC-coach wondered where this was going. These ideas seemed way overhead on the macro-economic level, instead of focusing on the business itself.

"Little did they know that eighty years later we would be having the same discussion again," Mr. Jones continued. "Of course you're now wondering what this has to do with KPIs." His green eyes twinkled below thick brown eyebrows.

"You took the words right out of my mouth," the ABC-coach said.

"I'll explain. The structure of most performance indicator systems doesn't stand the test of time. When change happens as radically as we see now, the foundation under our entire society becomes shaky at best. Values change. People appear to be in constant survival mode, taking impulsive actions to the detriment of others and eventually of themselves."

"How did you come to that conclusion? Your company and staff seem to be handling the latest recession pretty well."

"Yes, we prepared them for what was coming."

"How do you mean?"

"We had two guys called William Strauss and Neil Howe coming to the office for senior staff."

Mr. Jones reached behind him on the shelf. Out came a grey book with black stripes titled *The Fourth Turning*.

"I read their book way before 9/11, and it struck me that they predicted with some accuracy what was going to happen, to the U.S. and the world as a whole, at the dawn of the 21st century. Here's how they describe the current crisis: 'A decisive era of secular upheaval, when the values regime propels the replacement of the old civic order with a new one.'"

"And by new civic order they mean the foundation of our society?"

"Who are we to say that our business values will remain the same throughout such a global crisis?" Mr. Jones looked out his window, stared across the freeway to the vast spread of corn and wheat fields that lay on the other side. He especially enjoyed the time when the corn plants were at their highest, just before they were harvested. Their colors seemed to create a painting come alive, together with the blue sky and the sun.

"Here's the reality: we are in an economic winter, and a bad one. Nevertheless, some companies still make a profit; some markets are still growing and expanding. So the question remains: if you're not big enough to stay afloat in a huge storm without some sort of action, what can you do to avoid the killer waves?"

"I would say, use foresight as much as you can," the ABC-coach replied.

"Binoculars are a great invention," Mr. Jones smiled. "People are constantly on defense nowadays. But the best thing you can achieve when you're only playing defense is a tie."

"So what options do you have to counter this radical change?"

"Apple, by all accounts successful even though the economy is in a slump, has had the genius idea of demanding that their suppliers have a KPI measuring the number of hours their workers and bosses are trained and coached yearly. From what I understand, this is even more important than their turnover in most cases."

"So you're saying that by providing the right training and coaching tools on top of your KPI-structure, you'll more easily be able to keep the minds of your workers flexible?"

"Exactly. There's no revolutionary way of dealing with this kind of situation. You just try to maintain a level head. Understanding people's emotions will go a long way at such times."

The ABC-coach thanked Mr. Jones for his time and left his office. Passing people in the hall, she suddenly realized that the spark she'd noticed in people's eyes earlier was probably due to the fact that they had a natural interest in learning new things. She had seen it before in accomplished people she met on her journey.

When she arrived home she wrote three action items in her notebook:

1. Read up on patterns in economic history

2. Future pace based on those patterns

3. Use training time as a full-blooded KPI

Obfuscation vs. Ownership

Obscurum per obscurius – The obscure [explained] by the more obscure

~ Latin Proverb

"I want to tell you a story about a company I guided through a transitional period a few years ago, before I started working here.

"This was a company that created street signs for stores and brands. They were very good at it, had prime quality production assets and great personnel. They had been in business for more than thirty years.

"The founder of this company had three sons. One was very good at graphic design and was more of an artist, one was very good with numbers and customers, and one was very good at managing the production."

"I'd call that a golden combination of skills," said the ABC-coach.

"That's precisely what I thought. My question was: why do these guys want to hire me as a consultant? The numbers look great and they have a great staff. So what gives?

"Here was the kicker: the father sold one part of the company to each individual brother, so that all could benefit from his hard work. This collaboration appeared to be solid at first. The three brothers worked well together during meetings, and goals were being met.

"But after a while business started slowing down— it could have just been the economy that was going through a slump—and so they thought it was time to become more proactive in the market. They hired a top sales exec to bring in more clients, and paid him a fixed monthly fee plus commission."

"Did it work out?"

"Well, not exactly. That's why they brought me in. They wanted me to guide the sales exec toward more results. Unfortunately, the guy turned out to be dishonest, so they let him go."

"And what happened then?"

"I took one project that had been delayed for a while and focused all my attention on it. Everybody agreed that this project (worth several millions) was worth finishing quickly, so we agreed on certain deadlines.

"While everybody was putting the wheels in motion, I continued walking around the facility and listening to different staff members. I soon learned that obfuscation was the main strategy for the production manager in terms of motivating his staff of engineers. I didn't judge, at least not yet, about whether this was a good strategy or not."

"But, you didn't agree?" the ABC-coach wondered.

"No, but who am I to go about teaching people about honesty, I thought. I know better now." He smiled.

"So what happened to the project?"

"Well, after two weeks I got the confirmation that it was finished. So I jumped in my car, drove to the production facility and met with the key players there, so we could inspect the result.

"It turned out there was no result—we were about 50 percent ready. So I asked my clients why they were paying me to come over and inspect something that wasn't even finished yet. A silence followed. It appeared the strategy of obfuscation only lasted as long as the goals were not clear and the measurement was not done. As the saying goes, the proof is in the pudding."

"So what happened after that?"

"We agreed that they needed to clear up the business side of things before bringing me back in as an expert in marketing and sales. And so they did. One brother sold his piece of the company, and the two others continued without him. They are now growing again and providing top quality products for their clients with a speed that is unmatched in their country."

"So obfuscation only works until you get someone in place who actually cuts through the cloud of half-true explanations and politics," the ABC-coach said.

"Exactly so. And the reality is that politics are always involved. So 'owning' your KPI control circuit, in the sense that you live it, is essential. If you set a goal with your staff, hold yourself and them accountable."

"So what are the options for increased commitment and less obfuscation?"

"Maintain a limited and clear number of KPIs. Don't overuse KPIs to measure everything. Own them, don't use them as a way of saying, 'Hey, I've done my job, now it's your turn.' Lastly I would also suggest putting some sort of variable reward system in place, one that can be overhauled."

"But what about what Irving Fisher called the 'Money Illusion'? He said that no matter how many times you explain to people that bonuses can be withdrawn, they tend to interpret them as being irreversible."

"That's a good point. I have no answer for that. People are still people, no matter how much we educate them. But do you believe that paying someone too much for their contribution is worse than paying them exactly what they deserve?"

"Well, yes, I do," the ABC-coach replied.

"So why wouldn't we pay the right people for the right job the right amount of money, no matter what label we give the payment?"

The ABC-coach nodded and thanked Mr. Jones for his time. She had a lot to think about. As she left his office, she noticed a Post-it note on Mr. Jones's desk, and wondered what it was for.

Upon arriving home, she wrote three action items in her diary:

1. Define your #1 key result area, and create key-result-area specialists through on-the-job training

2. Watch out for any form of obfuscation to hide incompetence or unwillingness to grow

3. Minimize the "money illusion" by refusing to make bonuses a habit or a fixed pattern

Predictability vs. Post-its

"Forget it, Louis, no Civil War movie ever made a nickel."

~ Irving Thalberg's prediction to Louis B. Mayer regarding Gone With the Wind

"Have you ever heard the story about the guy who invented the Post-it?"

"No, I can't say that I have," the ABC-coach replied.

"Wikipedia says that the glue that makes Post-its so unique was invented by accident. Spence Silver, who is credited with being the inventor, was actually looking for a glue that would be ultra-strong, entirely the opposite of what Post-its actually do. The failed experiment that resulted in the glue used on Post-its was picked up by a guy looking for a way to hold his bookmark inside his chorus book while singing."

"So, it was an accident," the KPI-coach said.

"Well, yes and no. I would say there was some serendipity there, wouldn't you?

"The point is that the results of this failed experiment were very hard to predict. I mean, what are the odds of a guy singing in a choir and a failing scientist coming together with a product that would revolutionize the way we organize our offices?"

"And organize workshops," the ABC-coach added.

"That's right," Mr. Jones continued. "Think about the KPI-system Spence Silver was using. Did he in fact achieve his goal? No. Did he invent something with an irrefutable value to businesses worldwide? Yes!

"KPIs are a great system because they're an open-ended system. By definition, most businesses need this openendedness to thrive. Clients and their choices are the biggest unknown parameter that can determine the success or failure of a project.

"I like to remind myself of the Post-it story because, as we get older, we tend to start thinking more inside the box. The reality is that the success of our KPI cycle is predicated on its adaptability and the preparedness of the people to change their paradigms radically."

"But how do you deal with this when you analyze the data? Isn't that confusing? And what about people who miss their target, then use this argument as a reason why they didn't succeed?" The ABC-coach realized that any employee could use this argument to disarm a decision to reprimand or even fire them.

"That's where the Post-its really come in. We tend to think in one mainly-rational dimension when discussing numbers. I've learned that looking at the numbers in isolation from other factors can be misleading. I strongly believe that a well-developed intuition (some people actually call it 'thinking on your feet'), combined with analysis, provides much better results than just looking at the numbers.

"So what are some options you can use to make your system more flexible?"

"Always look for the Post-its in your business."

Suddenly both of them realized how silly that would sound to an outsider. The ABC-coach started laughing and so did Mr. Jones. As a matter of fact, as long as the ABC-coach could remember, Mr. Jones had always had one Post-it stuck on the back of his inbox, visible to whoever was on the other side of his desk.

"I see you noticed the Post-it." Mr. Jones chuckled. "Tell me honestly, how long have you been thinking of asking me why it is there?"

"Well, about a week ago I noticed it and I wondered why it was there. But I suppose it could have been in your office a lot longer."

"Every time I enter my office I walk up to this little yellow Post-it thinking: 'There is a need out there that needs to be filled. All it takes is the synergy between two ideas to create a new one.' And then I go out looking for those two ideas. I see them everywhere; the more KPI numbers I crunch the more they tell me a story.

"Also, when the number becomes predictable, get worried. Something is amiss. Numbers can be going up or down, but when the KPIs stop telling new stories it's time to ruffle the feathers of some staff members, or even your own feathers. However safe predictability might seem in the short term, in the long run you end up being overrun by your competitors."

"So you're saying that in order to grow your business and your KPI control circuit, you need to retain a balance between some level of predictability on the operational and tactical level, and a Post-it mentality, constantly looking for new opportunities."

"That's exactly right."

The KPI-coach felt she had had enough information, and returned home. She immediately stuck a Post-it on her desk.

She wrote down three action points in her diary:

1. Look for the Post-it possibility

2. KPIs are an ongoing improvement process and should be reviewed yearly

3. Use your intuition when studying numbers—your brain will tell you more if you just listen

Quality vs. Quantity

Time is that quality of nature which keeps events from happening all at once. Lately it doesn't seem to be working.

~ Anonymous

"That's a predictable debate," the ABC-coach said. "This is something that is discussed time and time again by many experts. The question is not which is best, or even which is most profitable, but we keep discussing these two things as though they were opposites instead of complementary and don't start making more money on both."

Mr. Jones seemed to be taken aback by this sudden outburst by the ABC-coach. He had gotten to know her as eager to learn but not too outspoken. After all, she was here to learn.

"You couldn't have put it more eloquently." he said. "After all, the two coexist in our market as we speak. It's just marketing."

Mr. Jones reached for one of the many books behind him on the shelves. He picked up a small book; it couldn't have been more than 100 pages.

"I remember reading this book named *Raving Fans*, written by Ken Blanchard and Sheldon Bowles a few years ago. The key message from the book was that to create fans of your business, your work, and of YOU, you should always

1. Decide what you want

2. Discover what the client wants

3. Do something extra (preferably one percent extra)

"So quality. . . quantity. . . blah, blah, blah." Mr. Jones exclaimed. "And this goes for internal clients as well as external clients. You decide what you want, you listen to the market, and you do something above and beyond."

"So you're saying that whatever you are selling, it's a matter of making a decision, discovering the client's reality, and creating options to give something more than the client expects."

"That's right. I've seen too many discussions on the value of this or that aspect of a product or service where one or both parties passionately tried to convince the other one that a certain aspect of a product or service had to be more 'qualitative' or 'quantitative' or, to put it bluntly, cheaper.

"Nobody wins and nothing changes with that sort of debate, no matter how lively.

"The reality is that analysis paralysis, feelings about how a vision lives within an organization, and opinionated rationalizing block the creative process from moving forward."

Mr. Jones put the book back on the shelf at exactly the spot from which he had taken it. The ABC-coach noticed how detail-oriented Mr. Jones was with his books. It was the third time she had seen him pick out a book and put it back exactly where it belonged.

"It all boils down to seven questions : How much time do you have to deliver? How big are your resources? Can you afford to spend a lot of money or not? What level of politics is involved? How much energy do you have to put in deciding what you want? How much in discovering what the client wants? And how much in extra service?"

"All of which are measurable aspects of a decision." the ABC-coach added.

She felt she knew enough. This was one topic that Mr. Jones was not prepared to spend much energy on. Both she and her mentor obviously felt that a decision should be reached quickly. A kind of "Say yes, figure out how later" attitude.

When she arrived home, after ordering the book on Amazon, she wrote down three action points:

1. Help people decide quicker and try new things

2. Avoid discussions on quality vs. quantity, as they are mostly emotional anyway

3. Build indicators on time spent in meetings and correlate them to the magnitude of results

Restriction vs. Reward

In nature there are neither rewards nor punishments. There are consequences.

~ Robert Ingersoll

"What is the goal of working with any sort of performance system in a business?" Mr. Jones asked.

"Well, that depends. It depends on the level of responsibility you have, the number of people you lead and manage, the business activity your company has—lots of variables," the ABC-coach responded.

Mr. Jones nodded. "The reality is that most people—especially people with little influence in their organization—first see the restrictions that come with working with a performance system. Only after a while do they see the rewards. With regards to causality, KPIs still have a lot to prove to people who just like to do their job and live their dreams elsewhere—and no, not just in front of the television. Actual dreams, like coaching your kid's soccer team as a way of seeing them grow up, or playing that musical instrument you always wanted to learn how to play.

"You see, managers and managerial systems don't control performance; people control performance."

The ABC-coach understood where this was going. "So what you are saying is that changing behavior does not necessarily mean that it changes people. And because we only measure the results of people's behavior and not the way they think, there is a flaw in how we use KPIs as a means of enforcing behavior."

"Yes, we are not Pavlov's dogs."

Yet again it amazed the ABC-coach how easy it was for Mr. Jones to just paraphrase what she said into one extremely short sentence.

"And yet, we are rewarding people for their achievements, knowing full well that if we keep doing it, eventually we will have to scale up our rewards because people get used to them. Rewards inflation, so to speak.

"On the other hand, we use KPIs as sticks to hit our employees with. Why do we do it? Because we need a legal framework in which to actively reward the top performer and to restrict (or fire) the bottom performers. And everybody knows this is how things work today. " Mr. Jones raised his arms in the air, looking up as if praying to the gods for common sense.

"Performance is supposed to inspire; therefore, performance indicators should do so, too. They should make our work easier. But the reality is that I cannot even tell you anymore how many cases of faulty use of KPI systems I have seen over the years. I still find it mind-boggling how humans and organizations alike are limiting themselves by focusing on what they don't want instead of what they do want.

"Correctly used, performance indicators bring clarity, broaden the scope of attention of managers to new ideas, and can create a healthy sense of competition across cultures or genders between the different players of the game that we call work and life."

"So what are our options?" the ABC-coach wanted to know.

"What about inclusion?" Mr. Jones asked. "Here's what Deloitte has to say about that: 'It is a business imperative to have different people of different genders, races, backgrounds in our organization.' A business imperative!" he exclaimed.

"Get people involved. Show your results, hold yourself accountable for successes and failures alike, get off your high horse and show you deserve your position. Educate people systematically about what KPIs can do. Look, we all use them—whether in our business or our life. The numbers are there when we want to see them."

"Doesn't that put you in a vulnerable position? Having your staff hold you accountable instead of you them?"

"As long as you keep the lines of communication going, it doesn't. As long as the relationship with your employee is based on trust instead of carrot and stick, it doesn't. Tell me this. How many times do you think someone without proper training and continuous education changes jobs in a lifetime?"

The ABC-coach considered the answer very carefully. She didn't know the exact number, but then it struck her. "There is no exact number nowadays. Every calculation done will prove to accurately reflect only a part of the workforce.

"But isn't that hard to measure?" she asked. "I mean, we can hardly predict where we are going to be in ten years, let alone in forty years or so."

"Yes, and you know what? I don't even want to know, because it would probably scare my socks off to realize how many of my employees will eventually end up having to go through the ordeal of looking for a new job every year or so because their function had become redundant."

"No doubt, and the speed of change is only increasing, so chances are our guesstimates wouldn't even be close to reality."

Upon arriving home, the ABC-coach thought deeply about what Mr. Jones had shared. He had a solid point: it's not about restriction or reward; it's about the perceptions of people.

She wrote three action points in her notebook:

1. Hold yourself as accountable for results as you would others

2. Results should never be at the mercy of age, nationality and/or gender.

3. Treat including people as a business imperative

Street-smart vs. Stubborn

Cunning or street-smart is not a burden

*~ based on a **16**th century author*

"So, do you think I am a stubborn person?" Mr. Jones asked the ABC-coach, looking her straight in the eyes.

"Well, I wouldn't say that you are stubborn per se."

"So what would you say instead?" Mr. Jones continued.

"Honestly, I would say you know what you want. You seem to be making your decisions based on the right information, and you follow up diligently." The ABC-coach really had no idea where this was going.

"Would you call me wise?"

"Yes."

"Great," Mr. Jones said. "But what does wise mean for you?"

"You seem to have a lot of experience in your field and you incorporate that into your daily activities."

"Wisdom is a combination of continuous improvement and experience." Mr. Jones said. "Some people would also call it street-smart."

"Where I come from, that's not necessarily a good thing. It depends on the street you grew up in," the ABC-coach smiled. She remembered growing up in a well-protected neighborhood, being able to play wherever and whenever she wanted. As she entered adulthood and started working with children from inner-city areas, she soon learned that there was a huge difference between their experience and hers that she had to overcome before she had any chance of making a lasting effect on their behavior.

"I grew up in a pretty normal family, but instead of taking the easy way of working in my father's company, I chose my own path. I made my first successes without being called 'Andrew Jones's son,' if you understand what I mean. My parents understood and supported that choice, even though they were somewhat disappointed that I would not immediately continue to build on their life's work."

"Yet here you are." The ABC-coach was brazen enough to mention that eventually Mr. Jones ended up running his father's company nevertheless.

"Yes, I decided to bring my accumulated managerial wisdom back to its roots. My goal now is to synergize the old way of doing things with my new way of management. It has been for years. Creating collaboration based solely on my ancestry would probably have been even more difficult than this way.

"The reality is that a lot of misunderstandings in using KPIs come from lack of a common language, and sometimes even the unwillingness to speak and understand the common language you have. And even though more students are studying longer than ever before, the gap between what I call the University of Hard Knocks and the ones that actually give you degrees has been steadily increasing.

"Considering what Ken Robinson said in 2006 on TED, I would say that we are not educated to become creative in whatever venture our life brings forth. Our education system sets us up to exist within a certain framework and use as little creativity as possible, no matter whether we're brought up under communism or capitalism. Isn't it strange that once we are a little intoxicated, our language skills seem to improve all of a sudden? It's as if our creative side comes alive. The truth is, it has always been there; it just lay dormant because we were scared to use it."

"So you mean fear is instilled within students."

"Precisely. The fear of making mistakes, of trying new things outside the safe zone of what society wants us to do, the fear of the unknown.

"Teachers don't consciously do that, of course. The education system itself always strives toward academic excellence—which in itself is a good thing, because you want people to succeed and thrive. Nevertheless, in a rapidly changing society like ours, because degrees always lose value even quicker than technology, sifting through the layers of academic performance to spot a potential star has become increasingly difficult and the risks involved in hiring the wrong person have become higher."

"What do you mean, degrees lose value?" The ABC-coach didn't really understand what Mr. Jones meant by that statement.

"Well, imagine you have too many people with a mechanical engineering degree coming out of college or university and not enough jobs for them. If you were one of those graduates, what would be the best way to increase your possibility of finding a new job?"

"Probably additional training and some hard work in sending out resumes."

"That's right! So the only way to increase your chances of finding a job, besides résumé-sending frenzies, is studying longer and getting a higher degree. Imagine that about 85 percent of the people have that very same idea. What would happen?"

"Business would get better educated employees."

"Ah, but would they be experienced?" Mr. Jones asked, crossing his arms over his chest and leaning back in his chair.

"No, I don't see how."

"Of course they wouldn't be. Most of them—not all of them—would end up feeling more confident and maybe even a bit cocky because of the hard work they've put into their education. They would be very hard to educate because they think they know so much. I would call that stubborn. Good for middle management, less so for top management where you need a natural interest in people, as well as political savvy."

"So what are the options for dealing with the language issue and the value depreciation of university and college degrees?"

"It all boils down to how you structure your HR department and policy. The goal is to find a good balance between street-smart people and higher-educated people and become the oil in the machine instead of the engine."

"And you can measure that by means of. . ." the ABC-coach wanted some more information on how to quantify that specific Key Performance Indicator in the organization.

"KPIs, of course. One that I particularly like is what I call 'Internal Client Satisfaction.' We do a quarterly anonymous survey on how all our employees like working with their co-workers. We then measure our own KPI, number of actions taken, based on those results."

"I see. And so it becomes a continuous cycle for everyone in the company."

The ABC-coach thanked Mr. Jones for his generous time.

When she arrived home, she wrote down three action points:

1. Study the academic inflation phenomenon

2. Speak the language of the people you work with

3. Do internal surveys on satisfaction

Tabula Rasa vs. TLC

Tabula Rasa (noun)
Definition from Merriam Webster's Online Dictionary:
1 : the mind in its hypothetical primary blank or empty
state before receiving outside impressions
2: something existing in its original pristine state
Origin: Latin, smoothed or erased tablet

"The ultimate goals of KPI implementation ought to be to develop potential in your organization, care for the people that work with and for you, and structure your business in a way that makes sense." Mr. Jones started the interview with this statement.

"Could you go into a little more detail?" the ABC-coach asked.

"First of all, you don't start a business or get into management when you don't want to push the boundaries of your knowledge and achieve some of your potential. Most big companies nowadays have some sort of 'hire-and-fire' policy when it comes to graduates. Some of these graduates make it, some of them don't. If they don't develop according to the curve set forward, you let them go, knowing full well they might become competitors or even more expensive contractors for you later on."

"And your internal guidelines give them measurable results they can work toward," the ABC-coach added.

"Exactly. But that doesn't mean you don't care for them, or, in a sense, take care of them. Exactly the opposite is true. I strongly believe that a good leader can only be proud of whatever accomplishments an employee achieves, within the boundaries of his organization or outside of it. You don't care HOW they make it, as long as they are successful at what they do."

"So in a sense, the organizational structure you create needs to build both your business and the people inside."

"Yes," Mr. Jones agreed. "Unfortunately, most KPIs in our organization never go deeper than behavioral changes on a basic level. They don't change how people think. Also, the reality is that ambitious people have a certain impatience for too much accountability. And they are right not to be too patient with us managers."

The ABC-coach smiled slightly at Mr. Jones' remark. "How do you mean, exactly?"

"Do you know how to measure managerial experience?" Mr. Jones asked.

The ABC-coach knew full well by now that Mr. Jones was never too impatient to wait for a well-thought-out answer. The first thing that came to mind was the number of years in management, but that was a dead giveaway, so probably it was something else altogether. She tried: "The number of bosses above you that have come and gone."

"Wow, you are sharp, aren't you? The number of palace revolutions you have been through in management. And as a consequence, the number of ambitious plans and KPI-revamps you've had to implement. The number of senior executives you've seen come and go.

"And that's where 'tabula rasa' comes into play, because most of these senior executives come with their ambitious plans to reach this or that goal and want to give the company a complete makeover to achieve that goal. They want to start with a clean slate.

"I like to paint," Mr. Jones said, "and I know from experience that once your painting starts to come to life you just want to improve it all the time. At a certain point, you start to feel frustrated because the painting just doesn't get finished and you don't know how to make it even more beautiful—for whatever reason. So the natural thing to do is to stare at the picture, hang it on the wall in a frame and look at it daily until you find that one aspect you're still missing. The other option is to start over by using white paint to erase all the work you've done. Which do you choose? Do you go Tabula Rasa or do you use TLC until you find that one action to make it perfect?"

"And by TLC you of course mean Tender Loving Care?"

"Yes, but you could use what Loral Langemeier describes as Team, Leadership and Conditioning, which is the business acronym."

"So, what are your options?" the ABC-coach asked.

"When you go Tabula Rasa with your KPIs, you will have to 'sell' the new program internally after having spent enough time listening to all levels in your organization before you start developing a new KPI-structure. You will have to show that the new structure will provide more value to your staff and bottom line, and create awareness before implementation.

"And above all, provide value to your internal clients— your staff. Be available to them during a big change process, reward them by whatever means you deem appropriate, and explain to them that the number of palace revolutions they go through teaches them what they don't teach you in school: experience."

Mr. Jones rose from his chair, shook the ABC-coach's hand and said, "And showing a little wisdom now and then also helps."

While driving home from the interview, the ABC-coach kept wondering where you draw the line in the sand when it comes to creating entirely new structures in your organization.

She wrote three things in her diary:

1. Take enough time to commit people to your cause. People want to buy in when they don't feel as if their hand is being forced.

2. Provide infinite value to your team and staff by maintaining a positive mental attitude—especially during a change process.

3. Know when you are stuck and apply either the 'white paint' technique or the 'painting-on-the-wall' technique to start over.

Ulcers vs. Upper Crust

Move upward, working out the beast,
And the ape and tiger die

~ Alfred, Lord Tennyson

"Have you ever had ulcers?" Mr. Jones asked the ABC-coach.

"Well, no, I can't say I have." she replied.

"Trust me, they hurt," Mr. Jones said simply.

"Doing business just is not worth having so much pain. Imagine yourself having a five-star restaurant. You have proven you are successful by all objective parameters: your food is obviously great, your staff is great, your service is amazing, you are revered as an upper crust chef.

"All of a sudden, you lose two very close friends, younger than you, who also own a restaurant. You have shared most of your time as chefs together, all becoming successful. You are left to wonder, 'Is it all worth it?' while you attend their funeral." Mr. Jones sighed and slumped back a bit in his chair, remembering losing some of his colleagues at an early age, before they were able to even begin to achieve their potential.

"So the question becomes different? You are saying that when you have blind ambition, ulcers (or some other health challenge) become unavoidable."

"Yes," Mr. Jones said. "We always work toward deliberate extremes, pushing ourselves as managers, and as human beings, to achieve more than our ancestors. But do we manage our personal KPIs like HDL cholesterol, energy level, bodily acidity, food and drug intake, the times we go out on vacation or do sports, as well as we manage our business KPIs?"

"So you're saying we think of measurable results as a must in our business and as a nice-to-have in our personal lives?"

"Not only that, but we tend to act as if our health is only urgent when something is wrong with it. Honestly, if I don't do any forecasting, my business doesn't grow. The same with your body: if you don't forecast, you get ulcers or worse.

"I remember my physical therapist telling me once we do more maintenance on our car's engine than on the engine that runs our body, our heart. Isn't that amazing? We give more attention to making our car run for another year than to keeping our heart running an extra year. And why?"

"So what are our options?" the ABC wanted to know.

"See the whole picture—not only your business, but the entire wheel of life, including your health, finances, social life, psychology, and your contribution to your friends, family and neighbors. Always be aware that using key results areas is not just a good business practice; it's a good life practice."

"So you're saying that joining the upper crust requires more than just working toward your next ulcer? I remember the late Jim Rohn always saying, 'Work harder on yourself than on your job.'"

"That's exactly what he said!" Mr. Jones exclaimed. "The reality is, however, that we get sucked into the details of our work, and that changes in our health mostly happen gradually. Besides that, most of us are programmed not to like working, whatever that may mean. So working on yourself is just as annoying as working on your job."

"Yes, and we always want to avoid continuous pain, so we are tempted to have ambition up to the point where that ambition really starts to create some pain or discomfort. Then we back off a bit, and that's where our ambition makes a place for ulcers because we seem to be 'stuck.' So coaching KPIs has as much to do with personal goals as it does with business metrics."

"Exactly, it's all just numbers."

"But how do you measure quality?"

"The same way you measure quantity. You see, everything can be brought back to numbers of some sort. As Kathy Casey, the Olympic figure skating coach once said, 'Great coaching and good intentions are not worth anything unless the goal is correct.' The mathematical analysis is like turning on a light in a dark room."

"In other words, find a way that works for you by studying different methods and adapt them," the ABC-coach said.

"Yes. In our next few interviews I'll show you the value of adaptation and having an open-ended KPI structure to coach with."

With this the ABC-coach left the obviously busy Mr. Jones. Upon arriving at her office she wrote down three action points:

1. To avoid ulcers, define personal goals as well as business goals

2. Create discomfort once in a while

3. Define indicators for all aspects of your life

acuum vs. VIP

Nature abhors a vacuum. When a mind lacks knowledge and flexibility, nature fills it with politics.

~ Harmen Stevens

"How are we ever to reach the stars if we don't travel through the biggest vacuum known to man?"

"How do you mean?" the ABC-coach inquired.

"The universe holds the stars. In order to reach them, we will have to travel for a really long time through a seemingly endless void. In business it's not that different. We sometimes go through periods feeling disconnected from our peers and our staff. In spite of this, we continue to grow as an organization. Then, all of a sudden, someone steps up, and a new star or self-proclaimed VIP is born. Consequentially, as we travel through a vacuum, new stars are born all the time—and other stars die."

"So the reality is. . ."

"The reality is that leading a business is sometimes very lonely. You do your best to get a functioning communication structure including KPIs in place and to inspire your staff to keep moving forward. But most of the stars are born no matter how much effort you put into developing one. It's just a matter of seeing them in that big vacuum we call a business."

"So it seems there are no real options to develop stars; it's only a question of finding them. But what options do we have for seeing them sooner?"

"Most of them are very practical in nature," Mr. Jones said. "Walk around. Walk around your company. Go to every production facility; talk to as many people as you can; ask as many questions as you can. Stars are everywhere. 'Go boldly where no man has gone before,' to quote a famous science fiction television series.

"Also, in talking to as many people as possible, remember how to win friends and influence people. Make people feel important and they will act accordingly. Make them feel dumb and you will create idiots."

"So what is a good time to walk around and meet people?"

"Any time is okay. Just don't make it structured. Go at nine in the morning, then three in the afternoon, then maybe 11 in the morning. If your employees work night shifts, go visit them at two in the morning. Most bosses don't leave their homes after midnight, but I believe they should. There is a certain special sense of pride that exists within people that work night shifts. Come in on Sundays if you have a weekend staff." Mr. Jones clearly felt very passionate about this subject.

"Early in my career," he went on, "I worked a trial night shift in a convenience store because I wanted to feel what it was like. I was taking over a franchise later that month and I wanted to know what my employees would be going through. The young man that helped throughout the night showed me how different communication with stressed and tired people actually is. I was stubborn (as some VIPs can be), trying to explain some rules to people in my own way, but I just didn't seem to get through—I was in a void and I knew it. This young man explained to me that using one sentence made everything clear to the customer. And you know what? I made a lot of mistakes in my counting that night. More than I ever did in my entire career. My KPI was off by ten percent, when 2.5 was the accepted margin of error."

"Why do you think that was?" the ABC-coach asked.

"The young man explained to me that it was actually quite normal to have a deviation from your normal performance. And also that it was quite normal that people don't understand things no matter how many times you explain them. And since I wasn't used to working nights, I spent too much energy on the wrong thing. At the end of the day my turnover was the most important aspect, and I failed to achieve that goal."

The ABC-coach thanked Mr. Jones for his input and walked out. Upon arriving at home, she wrote down three action points to remember to vindicate your KPIs:

1. Walk around your company premises at irregular times to see what's real

2. Listen to your employees to hear what's real

3. Understand what's real (your KPIs) and what's not (politics)

ater vs. Whatever

Life is really simple, but we insist on making it complicated.

~ Confucius

"Have you ever heard the term *'mind like water'*?"

"Isn't that something that meditation teachers aim for?"

"Yes, and it takes an immense discipline to actually achieve it," Mr. Jones said.

The ABC-coach grinned. "And did you achieve it?"

"No, I never did," Mr. Jones admitted. "However, in my search for a mind like water I met some very interesting ideas on how to achieve it that are not necessarily in the esoteric realm."

"How do you mean?"

"Well, I used to be a real chaos lover. I have a firm belief that from chaos can come creativity. That held me back, because I was too fanatic in maintaining that chaos in my office. Frankly, it was a mess."

"So what made you change your mind?"

"It all started when I read some books on time and project management. It appeared there was a consensus on the idea that you cannot manage time, only yourself. And to achieve a mind like water, it seemed a given that you've got to change your thinking from 'Whatever' to something a little more focused. You have to remember, I was a young boy back then and still in that phase where you are more into partying than doing things seriously."

"So what happened?"

"I cleaned out my desk and visualized how my ideal office space should look. After that, I started implementing a lot of changes really quickly. I started off with moving my office to a better energy workspace, selling all my office furniture, and keeping only my most essential and current project information nearby. I implemented a clean desk policy that has become a habit by now, and I expect ALL of my staff to have the same discipline. I even go as far as to ask them to bring me a picture of their home office, where they sit when they pay their bills and work on administration.

"It's unconventional, but it works. If people are dishonest, it's easy to spot. They bring a picture of a beautifully organized desk, and yet at work they cannot maintain the same level, so they're out even before their trial period is over."

"So you keep only those people who have had the discipline to keep their desks perfectly clean. Don't they lose creative momentum then?"

"That's why we have the Da Vinci room."

"The Da Vinci room?"

"It's a room where there are only three rules: it's a criticism-free room; you leave your ego at the door; and you enter barefoot."

The ABC-coach laughed at this remark. However, Mr. Jones remained unmoved. He was dead serious.

"Years ago, I met with a yoga specialist. She told me that by connecting myself directly with the ground, I could maintain a higher energy. And guess what? It works. Once I got hooked, it became something I didn't even think about anymore. I just did it whenever I felt like it, and I still feel great about it nowadays. And so does the staff. They even enjoy the process and ask me if they can walk barefoot into my office sometimes.

"The reality is that we cover most of our bodies with clothes nowadays, especially at work and most especially our feet. Our feet are practically always covered. In order to go back to the old way of contemplating new ideas around the campfire that is our meeting room, we need to show more of ourselves, not less."

"So what you're saying is that by breaking the patterns in your company, you break the patterns in the minds of the people and they perform at a higher level."

"Precisely. An environment that brings balance creates a difference in people, bringing them from 'Whatever'-state to 'Mind like water'-state. And then connecting with the biggest energy source you can find so you move forward with more creativity than ever before."

The ABC-coach shook Mr. Jones' hands and went home. She took her shoes off and started writing in her spiral notebook.

1. Focus on a 'Mind Like Water' work environment

2. Walk barefoot sometimes

3. Find a creative historic figure and rename meeting room

Xerox vs. Xylography

And never did a Grecian chisel trace,
a nymph, a nyad or a grace,
of finer form, or lovelier face!

~ Walter Scott

"Tony Robbins mentions that one of the key human needs is to feel unique, special and important." Mr. Jones was on a roll. His body language reflected his enthusiasm. His facial expressions were more vibrant than the ABC-coach had ever seen before. His hands were moving all over his desk, and his eyes betrayed a passion that the ABC-coach had not seen before.

She had a feeling that the final three letters of the alphabet were going to be spectacular.

"I hardly dare ask, but what do Xerox and Xylography have to do with KPIs?" the ABC-coach inquired.

"We live in a copy-and-paste society. Most of what we do in our business or personal life is a copy of what someone else has done before us—our parents, our peers, our colleagues at work, our predecessor in our function, our boss. Some people like this because it gives them certainty that they are functioning well. They are comfortable. There is consistency in their lives."

"So what you are saying is that we tend to just do what someone else has done before us because it's the safest and fastest route."

"Yes, and it doesn't help!" the manager exclaimed. "Ask any engineer: if you make a copy of a copy, there is always some quality loss. It might not be visible to the naked eye, but trust me, it's there. It's the same with KPIs. Just copying them means loss of quality, because the speed of change limits the validity of the KPI to the time (and place) of the emulation."

"How do you mean?" the ABC-coach asked.

"Well, let's say you take client satisfaction as a key measure. You take the same question: 'Are you very happy, happy, satisfied, not satisfied or not at all satisfied with the manner in which you were served at XYZ?' for another location called UVW.

"In some areas the term 'very happy' will mean exactly that: 'very happy.' But in other regions 'Satisfied' actually equals 'very happy.' It's a cultural and demographic thing."

"So, how do you deal with these local deviations?"

"You sculpt. Just like the art of xylography. Imagine you start with a large block of wood. At first you carve away big pieces, so that the piece of wood gets to a certain form that matches roughly with your desired outcome. Then you use finer tools to start working on the details. And in the end you use an ultra-fine chisel to chip out all the little pieces of wood that you still think are in the way. Sometimes it's even necessary to break out the sandpaper."

"I love the metaphor. So how do you translate this to KPIs?"

"You work harder at sculpting the indicators. There are three things to keep in mind as you do this :

"First, do a thorough statistical analysis based on both averages and standard deviations and variance.

"Next, start with a big enough block of wood. Start with all the numbers in your department and picture them to be perfect. Then start looking at the numbers one by one, asking questions: 'Does this make sense? What do I need to do to change them? In what order?' Start with one KPI and then go to the next.

"Finally, use technology that fits your organization. I have said this many times, but I know of too many consultants who try to implement new technology as a means of upselling. It annoys most managers because the technology is sometimes unfinished, unusable and unattractive to look at—making it hard to sell it to their staff even when management is convinced of its value."

"Is there some ideal KPI chisel you would recommend?" the ABC-coach inquired while frantically writing down what the manager was telling her.

"Yes, your staff."

"How do you mean?" the ABC-coach wanted to know.

"Well, use outside feedback for clarifying where you want to go (to help define the picture you want to create) and ask for internal feedback on how it looks while you are developing it."

"So your staff is your chisel."

"Yes, exactly. You can even give your staff a part to carve out when your trust level is high enough and politics are not playing too big a role."

"So in conclusion: copy-and-pasting an existing model only causes loss of quality even though it's faster. Chiseling out your own KPI model takes time but guarantees a better finished product."

The ABC-coach was baffled yet again by the simplicity of the hands-on approach the manager took to measuring results. She began to understand the meaning of common sense in developing KPIs and also the benefit of taking your time or your resources in order to achieve the right result for your business and department.

"So what would you recommend I coach people on when I start working with them?"

"Three things again: adopt a learning attitude instead of a teaching attitude. Most people love to show their expertise in their field of work. Second, explain to them that future pacing is key to building a good KPI cycle. And third, help them to keep KPIs sweet and simple."

The ABC-coach felt she had gathered more than enough applicable knowledge during this interview.

Upon leaving the manager's office, she passed a copy machine printing out dozens of copies at a time, realizing that most of these copies might have looked great but were still losing quality. It was a scary thought that a lot of businesses were still stuck in this copy-and-paste behavior, creating intangible costs for their organization, losing cashflow and not knowing why.

She went home, poured herself a hot chocolate, and wrote three things in her notebook:

1. Immediately eliminate redundant structures – you are too small to carry their weight around

2. Simplify KPI-matters to a maximum of three core KPIs – no more

3. Rely on your staff to bring you knowledge, not just information

Yours vs. Yankee

The house shows the owner.

~ Latin proverb

"When you look up Yankee in the history books, you might end up a little confused." Mr. Jones said right after the ABC-coach entered his office.

"At first it referred to the Dutch colonization force that landed in America early in the 18th century. Strangely enough, Jan (pronounced Yawn) and Kees are Dutch names that are still used today."

"So what does this have to do with KPIs?" the ABC-coach asked.

"Well, as a US citizen I always thought that mass management was strictly a U.S. specialty, developed early in the 20th century. While that is true, you would be surprised how many international companies actually adopt some form of Key Performance Indicators in their organizations."

"So why is there no real global standard that actually works in every industry, across all borders?"

"Oh, but there are scores of global standards. Industrial Standard for Organizations is one of them. I like ISO because it helps me keep focused on my client satisfaction and therefore my revenue-generating activities. Therein lies the problem: because of all these different standards, many companies are overwhelmed by an increasing number of quality reporting tools that look great in theory but need at least cultural adaptation, and sometimes even total revision."

"So the challenge of KPI coaching is that you actually need to translate, adapt and adjust what analysis tools you have at your disposal to match the reality of day-to-day business in your client's organization?" The ABC-coach looked a bit baffled at this point. She had believed that once you came into a company as a KPI expert, all the numbers would have been in place for you to start coaching immediately.

"Here's the thing," Mr. Jones continued. "In the U.S. we have assimilated so many different cultures into our organizations, that communicating about KPIs has become increasingly difficult. Try explaining a bad customer-satisfaction KPI to a Mexican woman or to a German man. Multiply that difficulty level by the number of management layers in your organizational structure."

Mr. Jones smiled a little, thinking about the time when he first realized how difficult communication about KPIs actually was the first time he addressed his staff.

"Yes, I can see that might be a bit difficult. Germans are a bit more interested in the process and want to start analyzing, and Mexicans sometimes get a little more emotional about both good and bad news."

"Yes, and it's the same with the Punjabi, Australians, Chinese, French, Greeks, and Italians. They all have cultural sensitivities. I remember one instance where we measured the number of actions taken by management as a Key Performance Indicator for progress. In China we consistently got one action item per department, whereas in Belgium we had about 10 per department." The manager grinned at this point, knowing that the ABC-coach was going to learn an important lesson.

"So the Chinese were lazy? I find that hard to believe." the ABC-coach tentatively said.

"Still, the numbers don't lie." The manager looked at her with a huge grin. "Why don't you ask me why there was such a difference?"

The ABC-coach decided to play along. "Well, okay, why did the Chinese have so few points of action?"

"In China you lose face when you have too many points to work on. So you inevitably end up with a document that is telling you a partial truth and not putting forward the entire reality," the manager explained.

"So, what you are saying is that the number of actions should not be counted as a KPI in China?" the ABC-coach asked.

"There is no real straightforward answer," Mr. Jones replied. "Quantitative KPIs are sometimes telling you things not only about the company numbers, but also about its culture. Sadly enough, the reality is that KPIs are often based on a 'think global, act global' principle instead of commonsense 'think global, act local.' There is no room in the KPI structure for local deviations."

"And because of this limited wriggle room in your management system, you can only achieve mediocre growth at best, which by nature a company will achieve anyway." the ABC-coach observed.

The manager nodded. "Unfortunately, many of the projects—however well-meaning —tend to fall into the category of promising big things and changing very little outside of what I call the demilitarized zone of KPI growth."

The ABC-coach said, "So even though the intentions of the senior management may be to achieve a big change, the controlling mechanisms that their executive staff—or another level of staff —are putting in place are a possible foot on the brake. So how do you coach somebody who works with this kind of constraint?"

"You have three different options. First, you need to understand the differences and discuss them with the different levels in your organization. And don't be afraid to stick your neck out. After all, you're the expert in your culture. Then you start collecting best practices across borders and keep yourself open to the fact that they might provide structure. After all, wouldn't it be great to take information from another country and just reframe it to your own reality?

"And lastly, tweak the existing KPI-control cycle to match the local situation and communicate about it."

The ABC-coach interrupted, "Yes, but isn't that really hard? I mean, reframing and modeling are part of my portfolio because I'm a coach. But what about someone without any coaching skills?"

"Have you ever met a manager with no coaching skills?" Mr. Jones replied impatiently. "I expect my staff to be both coaches and coachees. If they lack the necessary reframing skills, I send them to a mentor to help them with these issues. There is always someone—a formal or an informal leader—who likes coaching people."

"So the question then becomes, 'Which KPIs need tweaking?' instead of 'Which KPIs are we going to kind of, sort of "forget" when we implement this new project?'"

"Yes," Mr. Jones said, "and this is something you can get your staff involved in."

The ABC-coach thanked Mr. Jones for his explanation and left the office, realizing that soon the interview series would be over and she would have to go out in the world, creating her own association alphabet from scratch.

She wrote the following three ideas in her spiral notebook when she got home:

1. Understand differences between cultures and adjust (there's no ego involved)

2. Make a habit of collecting and tweaking best practices on a monthly basis

3. Empower people to coach you as well as you coach them

Zest vs. Zombie

Zombie (noun)
Definition from Merriam Webster's Online Dictionary:
1: usually zombi
2: a person held to resemble the so-called walking dead;
especially: AUTOMATON
3: a mixed drink made of several kinds of rum, liqueur,
and fruit juice

When the ABC-coach reached the final letter in the alphabet, she was somewhat surprised to find the word "Zombie" written in big letters on the paper on Mr. Jones' desk along with a picture of what seemed to be called 'Resident Evil.'

She had seen some strange stuff from Mr. Jones, but this was probably one of the weirdest ideas she had ever come across in working with Key Performance Indicators.

Knowing exactly how this interview would play out, she immediately asked Mr. Jones, "So, what exactly does a zombie have to do with number-crunching your department?"

"Well, it's pretty straightforward. Have you never had the feeling that—when faced with the analysis of your business—life was just sucked straight out of you?"

"Well," said the ABC-coach hesitantly, "yes."

"I'm sure most of us have had that feeling at some time." Mr. Jones smiled.

"One night I came home and watched this movie called *Night of the Living Dead*. This is a movie where the life gets sucked out of humans by zombies. I thought, 'That's exactly how I felt this morning in the office!'"

Mr. Jones continued, "Unfortunately, I also reacted like a zombie when people came into my office asking me questions while I was in analysis-mode. It was as if I was somehow unable to connect to the emotionally intelligent part of my brain. So I grumbled and mumbled some answers to my staff, thinking to myself 'Why can't I just react like a normal human being?'"

"And of course, this lead to your staff thinking you were this grumpy old man with a bad attitude, right?" the ABC-coach said.

"Yes! And after a while, I noticed the fire went out with some of my newer staff members, which of course made me even more grumpy."

"And what happened to the older staff members?"

"They were extremely helpful in explaining to our younger staff what happened to me when I was in 'zombie mode.' Basically their message was, 'Avoid him. Steer clear. If you have questions come to me.' Which of course made me even more angry, because not only did I lose control over my own temper, but I lost control over my staff as well."

The ABC-coach paraphrased: "So your reality was now that you and your staff both lost enthusiasm even though the numbers weren't bad at all."

'Yes!" Mr. Jones exclaimed. "And it took a long time and a lot of hard thinking about ways to break this spiral. Especially since I zigzagged all the time between reporting the numbers to upper management and taking care of the staff dynamics."

"Interesting," said the ABC-coach. "So basically you felt a pull to both be analytical and inspiring at the same time. So what did you do to align both these challenges of your job?"

"Well, in order to remind me that going into 'zombie mode' was holding me back, I starting associating analyzing number-crunching with the word ZEST."

"I opted for this word because it refers back to the spirit in an organization. I realized that numbers can work FOR you or AGAINST you. You can look at great numbers and say, 'These numbers aren't real because they're too good. They must have been really bad to start with or—even worse—manipulated.'"

"So when you have a lack of zest in your business, people tend to think that an increase is actually a bad thing, but when you have sufficient zest they will actually be glad that the results are improving. And you can do both using the same numbers, depending on how you look at them and treat them."

"Exactly," Mr. Jones said. 'When you treat numbers with enthusiasm and translate that enthusiasm in your communication with your staff, they will help you reach your full potential. If you look at them only from a—for lack of a better word—managerial standpoint, they will be numbers, nothing else."

"So what advice would you have for people in management that are facing the brain-sucking issue?"

"Well, to put it plainly, get coached."

"Wow," the ABC-coach smiled. "You're giving me a lot of responsibility."

"We can all use a positive kick in the butt sometimes. I remember my first coach telling me at some point, 'Why don't you behave less like a gravedigger and more like a human being?'"

Mr. Jones continued, "Needless to say, I was flabbergasted."

The ABC-coached laughed, remembering her first coach asking her why she looked like the female version of the WWF superstar 'The Undertaker' when she was managing or talking about her department.

"Also," Mr. Jones went on, "it's probably a good idea to review your own associative alphabet once in a while."

"Any suggestions as to when would be a good time?" the ABC-coach asked, sensing Mr. Jones was up to something.

"None whatsoever."

By now the ABC-coach could spot when Mr. Jones was playing mind games.

"So, imagine you would have some suggestions. What would they be?" she insisted.

Mr. Jones started laughing out loud and said, "Now where did you learn that neat little trick?"

"Oh—I don't know. I must have picked it up during an interview somewhere." the ABC-coach grinned.

"I believe reviewing your associative alphabet is a matter of knowing when you need to revisit your old habits and values. So get back to your list whenever clarity, direction, and motivation or zest is needed for you or for your staff. Ideally, I would say every year at least once is a great way to keep track of your personal associative thinking."

"And if you have never made such an associative alphabet, where would you suggest to start?"

"Easy—with the letter 'A.' Knowing what your ideal outcome is, first check your reality, then define the options you can think of to go from the negative association to the positive and take action."

"And for that you would need a coach to help you steer clear of the negative associations you deal with in a time-effective manner." The ABC-coach was now finally grasping the concept.

"Thank you for your time. I've learned quite a lot from the time we've spent together," she said after they exchanged some jokes on how ABC-coaching was already spreading to different levels in the organization. She had noticed upon entering the office that even the receptionist now had an ABC-associative diary at his desk and how the way he answered incoming calls had changed in tone.

With this idea in mind, the ABC-coach left the office and went back to her beautiful apartment, looking out over a blue lake that had the sunlight fall into it as she entered. It had been a fantastic six months.

She wrote down in her by now quite filled notebook:

1. Break the pattern to scare away the zombies

2. Maintain a REASONABLE amount of control in your organization—there is no such thing as passive involvement

3. Use the GROW model for your goals: Goals, Reality, Options and What are you going to do?

Soon after that, she started coaching people on the ABCs of performance as well, and started writing her own book on the ABCs of coaching.

But that's another story altogether. . .

References and Resources

Allen, David, *Making it all work*, Penguin Books, ©2008

Anderson, Chris, *Free: the future of a radical price*, Hyperion Books, ©2009

Blanchard, Ken and Bowles, Sheldon, *Raving fans: a revolutionary approach to customer service*, William Morrow and Company, ©1993

Covey, Stephen M.R., *The Speed of Trust*, Coveylink LLC, ©2006

Goulston, Mark, *Just Listen*, Amacom Books, ©2010

Strauss, William and Howe, Neil, *The Fourth Turning: an American Prophecy*, Broadway Books, ©1997

Toffler, Alvin and Heidi, *Revolutionary wealth*, Random House, ©2006

About the Author

Harmen has personally managed many sales teams and customer service advisors in multinational companies like Volkswagen and on a local level with startups in different countries. He aims toward achieving maximum performance in the shortest amount of time. His personal mission is to maximize the potential in every person he meets. He helps them grow faster by passing on all the practical proven people skills and business ideas he and his team can find.

He is the author of "the Performance Alphabet", an information-packed story about a coach modeling a 21st-century business leader by interviewing him using the alphabet as a way of anchoring knowledge.

He is a high-energy speaker that speaks in different continents about various topics, mainly about intercultural communication and business. He is fluent in four languages and lives with his wife and two daughters in a rural village called Vlimmeren.

He has had many life experiences, dating back to being a clerk at a gas station in the beginning of his career, to working in a warehouse, being a school administrator and finally ending up living his passion when he began educating people on a global scale as a business performance coach.

His organization, Ubeon, has a vision of building business collaboration without borders.

Contact details for Ubeon:

Ubeon C.V.B.A.
Cederdreef 9/1
BE-9230 Wetteren
Belgium

www.harmenstevens.com

Made in the USA
Lexington, KY
09 April 2015